100 NATURE HOT SPOTS IN
BRITISH COLUMBIA

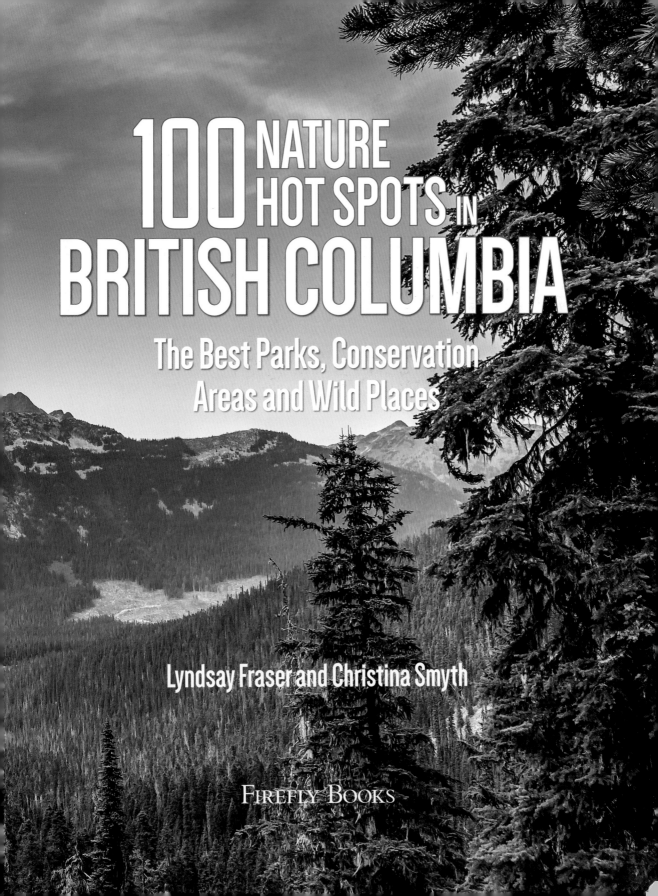

100 NATURE HOT SPOTS IN BRITISH COLUMBIA

The Best Parks, Conservation Areas and Wild Places

Lyndsay Fraser and Christina Smyth

FIREFLY BOOKS

A FIREFLY BOOK

Published by Firefly Books Ltd. 2018

First printing

Library of Congress Control Number: 2017957171

Library and Archives Canada Cataloguing in Publication
Fraser, Lyndsay, 1986-, author
    100 nature hot spots in British Columbia : the best parks, conservation areas and wild places / Lyndsay Fraser and Christina Smyth.

Includes index.
ISBN 978-0-228-10017-1 (softcover)

33614080705543

    1. Natural areas--British Columbia--Guidebooks. 2. Parks--British Columbia--Guidebooks. 3. Protected areas--British Columbia--Guidebooks. 4. British Columbia--Description and travel. 5. British Columbia--Guidebooks. 6. Guidebooks. I. Smyth, Christina, 1989-, author II. Title. III. Title: One hundred nature hot spots in British Columbia.

FC3807.F73 2018   917.1104   C2017-906833-4

Published in the United States by
Firefly Books (U.S.) Inc.
P.O. Box 1338, Ellicott Station
Buffalo, New York 14205

Published in Canada by
Firefly Books Ltd.
50 Staples Avenue, Unit 1
Richmond Hill, Ontario L4B 0A7

Cover and interior design: Kimberley Young
Maps: George Walker

Printed in China

Canada ▪▪▪ We acknowledge the financial support of the Government of Canada.

Dedication

To Marlyn, Lew, Tom and Olwen Smyth, who inspired me to explore British Columbia's natural spaces with wonder and confidence.
  —C.S.

To Mom, Dad and Kevin — growing up in a family that shared an inexhaustible enthusiasm for natural wonder and biodiversity undoubtedly led me to this place.
  —L.F.

Acknowledgements

We would like to acknowledge the First Nations of British Columbia who have lived on and cared for this land for thousands of years. It is through their sustainable practices, now combined with the efforts of the parks and other conservation and protection agencies, that these beautiful spaces continue to thrive.

While writing *100 Nature Hot Spots in British Columbia* we worked with and were supported by a number of people. A big thank you to our team at Firefly: Julie Takasaki and Ronnie Shuker for their enthusiasm and collaborative editing; Kimberley Young for her design; George Walker for his maps; and Michael Worek, Lionel Koffler, Steve Cameron and Ella Galpern for their ongoing support. We would also like to thank *110 Nature Hot Spots in Ontario* author Chris Earley for putting us in touch with our dedicated team at Firefly.

We reached out to a number of photographers and would like to thank all those credited on page 224 for sharing their talents. A special thank you goes out to Doug Fraser, who contributed numerous photographs and enthusiastically joined in on many adventures to explore new hot spots.

For their input and expertise during the writing process we would like to thank the following organizations: Parks Canada; BC Parks; Recreation Sites and Trails BC; the Burgess Shale Geoscience Foundation; Gwaii Haanas National Park Reserve, National Marine Conservation Area Reserve and Haida Heritage Site; Creston Wildlife Management Area; Dan Strickland; and UBC Okanagan.

And, finally, to the friends and family who supported us during our writing: Bryan Sexauer; Kala Draney; Elizabeth Young; Selene Rose; Kelsey Land; Chris Earley; Doug and Susan Fraser; Rob, Kara, Lochlan and Rylan Lemire; Bronwyn McNeil, Mila Cotic and the rest of the Science World family; and so many more. Thank you all for your support!

Contents

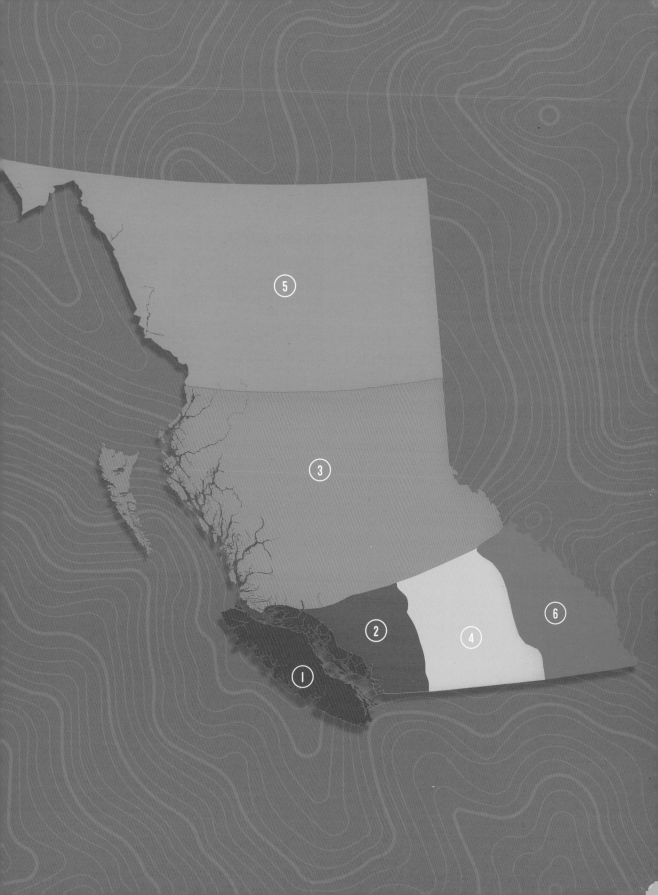

Introduction

Dominated by towering mountains and craggy coastlines, Canada's westernmost province is so geologically diverse that the nature hot spots found here are nothing less than abundant and varied. British Columbia is home to not only the driest, hottest place in Canada (Osoyoos) but also the wettest (Prince Rupert). From saltwater marshes to dry grasslands and coastal temperate rainforests to alpine tundra, the province's diverse climate and topography host an incredible array of life.

British Columbia is one of the best places in the world for viewing large mammals — massive grizzly bears gathering at rivers and streams for salmon feasts, humpback whales clownishly leaping and breaching in deep waters along the coast and bighorn sheep clashing their horns together in a valiant battle for breeding rights on mountain sides. That said, there is much more to the rich natural history here than large mammals. Of the country's 15,000 species of fungi, 10,000 are in BC. Over 500 species of birds have been recorded in the province, and nearly half of the country's reptilian and amphibian species can be found here as well. Many species of plants and animals, such as the Vancouver Island marmot and the hotwater physa, are endemic to BC, meaning they're found nowhere else in the world.

All of this translates to a province so naturally rich that there is something for everyone to enjoy, whether you're keen on wildflowers, lichens, mosses, fossils or other natural wonders. To protect it all, British Columbia has established the most extensive park system in the country, encompassing seven national parks, over 1,000 provincially protected spaces — which include parks, conservancies and ecological reserves — and countless regional parks and protected areas managed by local conservancies, land trusts, landowners and volunteer organizations.

This stunning province also covers the traditional territories of 198 First Nations who have lived on and cared for this land for thousands of years. The nations are diverse, and each carries different ecological knowledge and cultural traditions. Throughout the province, visitors may encounter up to 30 languages and tour many important historical sites, some of which date back over 10,000 years. Wherever possible we have shared First Nations' history as well as the original names for the places we enjoy.

We've organized this book by region to give you snapshots of some exceptional places to explore in different corners of the province. Some hot spots are a quick turn off a main road, while others are a little more challenging to reach. Whether it's a long drive down a logging road or a nautical journey on a ferry, we assure you all are worth the effort to get there! A number of hot spots are easily accessible to nature lovers of any ability, but some may require greater physical prowess and more extensive trip planning. Be aware of your own abilities and limitations and plan accordingly. We hope this book provides inspiration and insight as you design your own adventures, but we highly recommend you check park websites, weather forecasts, trail conditions and tide times, and take other relevant precautions for the site you're visiting. There are many fantastic websites and guidebooks with detailed descriptions of what to expect on hikes of all difficulty levels throughout BC.

While we ourselves are passionate explorers of this beautiful province, and hope you are too, we are also well aware of the environmental risks that come with increased human traffic to these areas. Shrinking wild spaces, increased pollution, a changing climate, human-caused forest fires and an ever-growing human population all play a part in impacting these sensitive ecosystems. We urge those who visit to be respectful of the amazing places we all have the privilege of exploring. In addition to getting out there and admiring these natural wonders, please support the terrific conservation programs run by your regional, provincial and national parks, not-for-profit organizations and other protection agencies. Their tireless efforts help ensure there are nature hot spots to cherish for generations to come.

Along with keeping these spaces safe from human impact, we want readers to stay safe themselves. Weather in the mountains can change quickly, tides can rise suddenly and trails may not always be obvious. Be sure to carry these 10 essentials whenever you are hiking: water, food, extra clothing, fire-starting materials, a light source, first-aid supplies, a communication device, a map of the area, sun protection and an emergency shelter, such as a tarp. Always carry bear spray in bear country, and learn how to stay safe during wildlife encounters with Wild Safe BC (www.wildsafebc.com).

Happy exploring!

These icons appear throughout to give you an idea of the available activities and features at each hot spot:

- 🖑 Hiking
- 🔭 Wildlife viewing
- 🚲 Cycling
- 🛶 Kayaking, canoeing or rafting
- 🏊 Swimming
- 🤿 Scuba diving or snorkelling
- 🏄 Surfing
- 🎿 Skiing
- 🎿 Snowshoeing
- 🧗 Rock climbing
- ⛺ Camping
- ♿ Accessible

Information regarding universal access has been taken from available data provided by each location. Please note that this data may refer to specific trails, parking or toilets at the hot spot, and visitors with accessibility needs may be unable to experience fully the highlights we profile. Please confirm the availability of accessible facilities and trails prior to departure.

Nature Hot Spots and Dogs
Given the delicate nature of many of these destinations, we strongly recommend that you leave your pets at home. Even the most well-behaved dogs are capable of disrupting a sensitive ecosystem, and their presence and excrement may attract dangerous wildlife or scare animals away, which could affect your wildlife-watching experience. If you wish to bring your dog, please contact the destination in advance to learn about limitations and any precautions you must take. Please obey all signs, dispose of your pet's excrement appropriately and take additional care when meeting other people and pets.

Queen Charlotte Sound

San Josef Bay 28

Port Alice 8

Sointula 2

Vancouver Island

19

Sayward 27

Campbell River 9 22

7

Lund

21

23

Powell River

Egmont

31

Comox 17

11

29 Sunshine Coast Hwy

10

19

14

4

16

Qualicum Beach 15

4

20 18

25 Parksville

Vancouver

5 Nanaimo

Richmond

Tofino 34 19

Port Alberni

30

36 6

1 Bamfield

Duncan

1

32

26 13

35

Port Renfrew 3

12 24

33 Victoria

Sooke 37

PACIFIC OCEAN

N
W E
S

Vancouver Island and the Coast

Bamfield

A sanctuary for marine life on the west coast of Vancouver Island

What Makes This Hot Spot Hot?

- Visitors can explore one of the most biodiverse marine habitats in Canada.
- Short hikes lead to views of migratory paths for thousands of whales.
- A world-renowned marine research station provides more information on the natural history of the area.

Address: Bamfield, BC
Tel.: N/A
Website:
www.bamfieldmsc.com

GPS Coordinates
Latitude: 48.82788
Longitude: −125.13427

Open year-round

 The Cape Beale Lighthouse is the first lighthouse on Vancouver Island.

Visit nearby tidal pools one day then camp on a remote sandy beach and visit a historic lighthouse the next, all while soaking in the beauty of a small ocean town. The most accessible beaches are a short boat ride across the Bamfield Inlet. A walk along an easy trail will lead you to Brady's Beach and Eagle Bay, where the shoreline hosts towering sea stacks surrounded by sand and rocky beaches. Explore tidal pools filled with a variety of sea stars, anemones and other marine invertebrates. Look carefully in these pools and you may see small, beautifully coloured sea slugs, such as opalescent nudibranchs, crawling upside-down on the water's surface.

A birding hot spot, this environment supports the marbled murrelet, an

endangered seabird that nests high in the trees of old-growth rainforests and feeds on ocean fish. The marbled murrelet is threatened by logging, and the beaches of Bamfield are one of the few undisturbed places with fairly easy access to view this bird.

For the more ambitious hiker, a moderate trail leads through old-growth temperate rainforest to Cape Beale. After venturing through a forest of lush ferns, mosses and towering cedars, make your way to Tapaltos or Keeha Beach. These expansive sandy beaches feature an abundance of rocky tidal pools, sea stacks and arching rock formations. Most people take day hikes to these beaches as the trek is approximately a 7-kilometre round trip. Others may choose to camp at Tapaltos then continue on to the Cape Beale Lighthouse, another 4.5 kilometres, the next day. Along this trail the forest slowly morphs into bogs, sandflats and windblown meadows with small, hardy trees. The rocky point upon which the historic Cape Beale Lighthouse is perched looks out onto the open ocean. Past the crashing waves grey whales are a frequent sight, particularly during the summer months.

↑ Keeha Beach makes a beautiful campsite, with rocky tidal pools along a sandy beach.

↓ Tidal pools are home to a wide variety of sea life including the giant green anemone.

Bere Point Regional Park

Old-growth Sitkas, cedars dripping with lichens and a smooth pebble beach that just might provide a chance to witness a unique orca behaviour

What Makes This Hot Spot Hot?

- Northern resident orcas are the only BC orcas to display beach-rubbing behaviour.
- Giant old-growth Sitka spruce can be viewed along a beautiful trail.
- Once your hike is finished, the nearby community of Sointula has much to explore and a rich history to share.

Address: Sointula, Malcolm Island, BC
Tel.: (250) 973-2001
Website: www.sointulainfo.ca/about-malcolm-island/bere-point-regional-park

GPS Coordinates
Latitude: 50.66618
Longitude: −127.05373

Open year-round

↗ **Skirted by dense salal, a redcedar nearly completely hollow from fire damage lives on.**

The aptly named Beautiful Bay Trail on Malcolm Island, just a short ferry ride from Port McNeill, offers stunning views of the Queen Charlotte Strait and ample opportunities for a nature adventure. The 5-kilometre trail first meanders through dense salal undergrowth so tall it gives the impression of a hedge lining the path. Beautiful sun- and wind-weathered Western hemlock and redcedars loom large, their trunks and branches dusted and dripping with various lichens. Farther down the trail the forest canopy thickens and the undergrowth opens up, as light reaching the forest floor becomes scarce. The path winds through a spectacular forest, offering glimpses of the sparkling bay. This pristine environment is home to a number of ancient Sitka spruce, which tower over their neighbours, the largest reaching heights of more than 60 metres.

Although a rare sight for the occasional visitor, one population of orca whales, the Northeast Pacific northern resident orca, is known to display a distinctive behaviour along this park's pebbly beach that is not performed by any other orca populations sharing BC coastal waters. Swimming right up to the shallow waters of the beach, these whales roll and writhe as they rub their bodies across the smooth stones.

The puzzling habit appears to offer no biological advantage; otherwise other local orca populations would be expected to share this trait. It is therefore believed to be

a cultural custom, unique to these whales. From the looks of it, it probably feels pretty good too. Although rare to see, you may choose to linger within view of the beach for some time just in case. To avoid disturbing these magnificent animals during their curious display, be mindful to watch for whales from the whale-watching platform along the trail and not directly from the beach.

Although a day spent at Beautiful Bay is worth the trip alone, plan to explore the rest of the island as well — the entire 24-kilometre length of it. Its notable history has led to its current charm: once populated as a utopian Finnish community, Sointula, meaning "place of harmony," has maintained many of its ideals of equality and cooperation. The island's co-op store is still used, over 100 years since it first opened, and be sure you pop into the resource centre when you first arrive for advice on how to make the most of your visit to this wonderful community. Be careful, Malcolm Island's wilderness and its friendly human inhabitants may steal your heart, making it difficult to board the ferry and say farewell.

↑ Round stones make for the perfect rubbing beach for the northern resident orcas.

↖ Orca whales frequent the waters around Bere Point.

JUAN DE FUCA PROVINCIAL PARK

Botanical Beach

This shoreline's remarkably diverse intertidal life provides an opportunity to witness some of BC's most fascinating marine fauna first-hand

What Makes This Hot Spot Hot?

- Tidal pools are home to extremely diverse varieties of species.
- To reach the beaches visitors can walk a beautiful temperate rainforest trail loop, which also connects to the Juan de Fuca Trail.
- There are opportunities to see marine mammals, such as orca whales, grey whales, seals, sea lions and otters.

Address: Juan de Fuca Provincial Park, BC
Tel.: (250) 474-1336
Website: www.env.gov.bc.ca/bcparks/explore/parkpgs/juan_de_fuca/trailhd.html#botanical

GPS Coordinates
Latitude: 48.534075
Longitude: −124.443427

Open year-round

↗ **These purple sea urchins use their sharp spines to grind out shallow cavities into the sandstone for a place to reside at low tide.**

A short walk through coastal temperate rainforest, a beautiful experience in itself, will bring you to the perfect spot to experience the diverse marine life of the Pacific Northwest. Protected within the boundaries of Juan de Fuca Provincial Park, Botanical Beach is the ideal spot for exploring the rich intertidal zone, the area that lies between the highest and lowest tides.

Botanical Beach is home to an abundance of life, so expect to see multiple species of crabs, snails, sea anemones, limpets, barnacles, sea urchins, mussels, chitons, sea stars and brittle stars, as well as the occasional nudibranch or sea cucumber. The crystal-clear tidal pools allow for perfect viewing, but take the time to carefully examine each one — you will be surprised at what comes to life. An unassuming snail shell may be home to one of several species of hermit crab, and giant green anemones may be seen using their stinging tentacles to catch a meal.

The marine life is fragile and the rocks can be very slippery,

so step thoughtfully — delicate snails, limpets, barnacles and other amazing creatures inhabit most surfaces, carefully enclosed in their shells to avoid desiccating while waiting for the tide to return. Plan your trip with the tides in mind, arriving at least an hour before low tide for time to explore the entire stretch of this family-friendly shoreline. The parking lot of this popular spot fills up quickly, so arriving early in the morning is best.

Botany Bay, an adjacent beach accessible from the same trail loop, is also worth

a visit for beautiful views of rugged cliffs and the black basalt shoreline. While the intertidal life is well worth the trip on all but the coldest days of the year, the area also offers opportunities for large marine mammal sightings — California and northern sea lions can be seen during the summer months, and harbour seals and river otters are also frequently spotted in the area. It is not uncommon for these shores to be visited by orca whales or even grey whales as they migrate north up the coast between March and April.

↑ The fascinating geology of this park has created unique viewing opportunities, as the sandstone has been carved away by wave-tossed rocks and boulders that grind uniquely smooth and deep pools into the shoreline.

Bowen Island

Life thrives in and around this small island community

What Makes This Hot Spot Hot?

- Visitors can get from seaside to lakeshore with a quick walk through the forest.
- The waters of Howe Sound are perfect to kayak or canoe around the island.
- A hike to a high point offers views of Vancouver and Howe Sound from a new perspective.

Address: Bowen Island, BC
Tel.: (604) 224-5739
Website:
www.tourismbowenisland.com

GPS Coordinates
Latitude: 49.37676
Longitude: −123.37015

Open year-round

↗ **Pileated woodpeckers can be spotted around the trails near Killarney Lake.**

A short ferry ride from Horseshoe Bay or a water taxi from downtown Vancouver will take you to this beautiful island situated at the mouth of Howe Sound. At just over 52 square kilometres, Bowen Island has both inland and ocean hot spots to tour. Steep shores make kayaking a good alternative for the ocean explorer, and kayak tours and rentals are available on the island. From the water you can view picturesque rocky shores and watch for the marine mammals that frequent these waters, from orcas and porpoises to sea lions and otters. (Of course, remember to keep a safe distance from these creatures.) Great blue herons and bald eagles are a common sight from land and water on Snug Cove and Deep Bay, just to the north.

For an inland hiking adventure, travel along the main road and follow signs for Killarney Lake on the Crippen Regional Park trails. A hike over rolling hills through cedar and hemlock forests leads to Killarney Lake, and the trails around the lake

offer boardwalks and scenic viewpoints. At the north end of the lake is a marshy area full of lily pads, algae and the stumps of old cedar trees. This environment is perfect for dragonflies and other insects, which attract insectivorous birds, making it an excellent area for birdwatchers. Pileated woodpeckers, red-breasted sapsuckers, pied-billed grebes and a host of other tree- and water-loving birds have been sighted in this area.

For a hike with a view head south after exiting the ferry and walk along the sandy beach of Snug Cove. A short but steep hike leads you through the forest to a lookout point. On a clear day you may see Howe Sound, Vancouver and the rocky shores of Bowen Island from a higher vantage point. No camping is permitted on this island, so be mindful of the ferry times, which change throughout the year.

↑ Seals enjoy the sunshine on a nearby rock at low tide.

↖ A boardwalk leads hikers through enchanting forests.

Bowen Park

A nature escape that brings coho salmon to the heart of a city

What Makes This Hot Spot Hot?

- This site provides wildlife viewing opportunities in central Nanaimo.
- Coho salmon now spawn in the Millstone River thanks to a human-made side channel.
- Interpretive trails allow for birding opportunities year-round.

Address: 500 Bowen Road, Nanaimo, BC
Tel.: (250) 756-5200
Website: www.nanaimo.ca/PRC/Locations/Parks/56-Bowen-Park

GPS Coordinates
Latitude: 49.173432
Longitude: −123.960510

Open year-round

 (Check ahead)

Even in the heart of a city natural treasures can be found, and a short walk into a forest can leave you shrouded in wilderness. The 35-hectare Bowen Park in the city of Nanaimo is home to beautiful waterfalls that become quite dramatic in late winter and early spring as the water levels rise. Watch for common mergansers diving into the rushing waters, and listen for the dramatic song of the Pacific wren — a tune so lengthy and complex, it is hard to believe it is coming from such a tiny, secretive bird, barely larger than a hummingbird.

Although the park is home to a playground, curling club, picnic area and recreation centre, do not let the bustling east end of this city park fool you, as there is lots of nature to be seen. For the best access to the trails and to avoid the busy facilities, use the park entrance off Wakesiah Avenue.

The interpretive trails of Bowen Park pass through the forest and trace the meandering Millstone River, where you can find a human-made side channel created to support the critically declining coho salmon, allowing them passage into the river. Stepping pools, fishways and an alternative path around Bowen Park's rushing falls allow the

⤸ The side channel created for coho salmon looks natural despite being a human-made addition to the park.

➧ A young barred owl watches the stream intently, looking for an evening snack.

salmon to continue upstream to spawn. Although it was a significant undertaking in the park, the development of this channel paid off almost immediately — the very day water was released into the newly developed side channel in 2007, coho began to use it. Now hundreds of salmon use this route, and local students raise and release salmon fry into the channel each year. The channel was so well designed that within a few years it looked as though it was a natural stream that had always been a part of this ecosystem.

A family of barred owls has been nesting in the park for years, and if you are lucky, you might get a chance to watch young owls learning important skills from their parents. The owlets can sometimes be seen at the river's edge being taught how to hunt for crayfish in the shallow water. After the owl family has split at the end of the summer, young owls may still be found in the area, demonstrating what they have learned from their parents earlier in the season.

Broken Group Islands

An archipelago within a national park protects an ocean paradise

What Makes This Hot Spot Hot?

- These unique islands feature white sand beaches, rocky shores and tidal pools.
- This is the birthplace of the Tseshaht First Nation, where you can discover many cultural artifacts.
- Ocean currents create a late-summer bloom of micro-organisms that turn the water bioluminescent.

Address: Main Access via Ucluelet, BC
Tel.: (250) 726-3500
Website: www.pc.gc.ca/en/pn-np/bc/pacificrim/activ/visit4c/activ4

GPS Coordinates
Latitude: 48.91905
Longitude: −125.28001

Open year-round, July and August are the best times to visit

↗ **Kayaking is a spectacular way to explore these islands.**

The Broken Group Islands are an archipelago of over 100 islands with white sand beaches, rocky shores, a rich Indigenous history and many opportunities for wildlife viewing. Visitors frequently spot seals, sea lions, grey whales and a variety of other ocean mammals. However, the biodiversity of these islands is really demonstrated in the intertidal zone by the marine invertebrates that inhabit these waters.

On Wouwer Island you will find the Great Tide Pool, which is large enough to swim in and filled with many ocean animals, including sea cucumbers, sea stars and moon snails. Visit at low tide for the best opportunity to get up close and personal with these creatures. If you are feeling ambitious and wish to take a dip, bring a wetsuit and a snorkel as the water is cold year-round.

The summer months bring an abundance of bioluminescent micro-organisms called diatoms. When disturbed these diatoms emit a burst of blue-white light. After the sun sets, run your hand through the water and watch it glow behind you. If you are lucky you may see a school of fish creating a moving ball of light beneath the ocean surface. Plan your visit in mid-August for the best chance of experiencing this natural wonder.

The Broken Group Islands are situated within the Pacific Rim National Park Reserve. Beachkeepers maintain the area and have a wealth of information to share with visitors. They may be able to point you towards culturally significant areas of the Tseshaht Nation, to whom this archipelago is of great importance. Benson Island, the birthplace of the Tseshaht, has an interpretive display featuring a traditionally carved house post. A guided kayak tour from Ucluelet is the easiest way to access these islands. For experienced kayakers another option is to rent a water taxi to carry kayaks to the islands and then explore the archipelago on your own.

→ **The shell of a moon snail.**

→→ **Seals bask in the sun on an algae-covered rock.**

Desolation Sound Marine Provincial Park

Stunning shorelines to explore, where the mountains meet the ocean

What Makes This Hot Spot Hot?

- The area has some of the warmest ocean waters north of Mexico.
- It is the largest marine park in British Columbia.
- Fjords create the perfect setting for exploring the coastline from the water.

Address: 32 km north of Powell River, BC
Tel.: (250) 286-9992
Website: www.env.gov. bc.ca/bcparks/explore/ parkpgs/desolation

GPS Coordinates
Latitude: 50.11232
Longitude: –124.68836

Open March to October

When Captain George Vancouver visited these waters in 1792, he deemed the shoreline so remote and inhospitable that he gave it the name Desolation Sound. He was partially correct, as the dramatic shorelines of this sound are inaccessible by car even today, but what was once considered an inhabitable and bleak wilderness is now an 8,449-hectare marine park and a paradise for nature lovers. The warm protected waters and dramatic scenery make it the perfect place to explore by water.

Desolation Sound Marine Provincial Park makes up the northern boundary of the Sunshine Coast, past the village of Lund, where the Sunshine Coast Highway ends. Long ago the huge valleys were slowly carved by ancient glaciers before becoming submerged by the rising sea. The resulting steep forested fjords of this marine haven are breathtaking. These coastal mountains ascend from the shore almost perpendicular to the sea, to heights of over 2,000 metres in some areas. The many inlets and islands create a seemingly endless coastline to discover at your leisure.

◂ Calm waters and seemingly endless fjords are the main attractions in Desolation Sound.

→ Along the rocky cliffs that rise directly from the sea, intertidal life is left exposed at low tide.

The narrows straits and passages of the area slow the tidal waves coming into the sound. As opposite tidal waves meet coming from the north and south, they create disordered and complex tidal patterns and weaken the tidal currents. This is what allows the surface water to stay extremely calm and the temperature to be comfortable in the summer, making the park a perfect place for exploring nature in the water, whether you are swimming, snorkelling, scuba diving, boating or kayaking.

Make sure you get in close to the shoreline as you explore the dramatic scenery. Giant sunflower stars, spiny rockfish, sea cucumbers, oysters and much more make up just some of the diverse intertidal life here. Purple sea stars can be seen clinging vertically from the rock faces as the tide recedes, while harbour seals sun themselves on the more gently sloped rocky shores.

ALICE LAKE LOOP

Devil's Bath and Eternal Fountain

Karst landforms surrounding Alice Lake have created Canada's largest cenote and a disappearing waterfall

What Makes This Hot Spot Hot?

- Visitors have access to views of Canada's largest cenote.
- Trails lead to the dramatic Eternal Fountain, which disappears into caves below.
- Karst windows provide views into the rushing water hidden in underground caves.

Address: Alice Lake Road, Mount Waddington, BC
Tel.: (250) 956-3301
Websites:
www.vancouverislandnorth.
ca/things-to-do/nature/
parks/alice-lake-loop-tour,
www.rdmw.bc.ca/regional-
services/parks/#1334

GPS Coordinates
Latitude: 50.395335
Longitude: −127.304254

Open year-round

Although the Alice Lake Loop is a rough, active logging road that should not be conquered without a truck, it is worth the rutted and potholed drive to witness impressive examples of the power of dramatically surging freshwater as it shapes the landscape.

With a circumference of 359 metres and reaching a depth of 44 metres, Devil's Bath is Canada's largest cenote, a sinkhole fed by groundwater. Photos do not do this colossal geologic rarity justice, so you will have to go see it yourself. Cenotes are often created when sections of cave roofs collapse, revealing a previously hidden cavernous system below. Cenotes and underground caves are typical features of karst landforms. This unique terrain commonly forms when limestone bedrock dissolves below the water table. Devil's Bath connects to the Benson River Cave through a submerged tunnel. At the surface trees cling desperately to the edges of the vertical cliff that drops down to the water far below, and in the calm waters of the sinkhole

◂ **A well-constructed lookout provides a view of the massive Devil's Bath below.**

▸ **A rush of water emerges and just as quickly disappears at Eternal Fountain.**

float giant logs of trees that lost their hold in days past.

Another stop along the Alice Lake Loop not to be missed is Eternal Fountain. This waterfall gives the impression of a fountain on a continuous loop: a powerful surge of water gushes from the rock face, falls nearly 5 metres into a moss-covered rocky opening in the forest floor and then disappears from sight. This type of waterfall is known as a resurgence, when an underground stream returns to the surface. The swallet, where the stream disappears back into the ground, flows through concealed caves below. Stay on the trails to avoid the risk of falling — with so many underground caves, there are hidden openings and unstable ground. Additional karst windows into this underwater course can be viewed just a short distance from Eternal Fountain, all nestled within a beautiful temperate forest backdrop.

Elk Falls Provincial Park

The Campbell River crashes down into a steep canyon enveloped by tranquil forest

What Makes This Hot Spot Hot?

- Elk Falls is an impressive 25-metre plunge into a large canyon.
- A new suspension bridge makes for better views of the falls.
- Five species of salmon spawn in the channels.

Address: Gold River Hwy (Hwy 28), Campbell River, BC
Tel.: (250) 474-1336
Website: www.env.gov. bc.ca/bcparks/explore/ parkpgs/elk_falls

GPS Coordinates
Latitude: 50.04094
Longitude: −125.31999

Open year-round

(Check ahead)

↗ **Viewing platforms and a suspension bridge let you experience the monumental rush of water from above the falls.**

As notable and distinguished as its namesake, the sight of Elk Falls' 25-metre drop is certainly worth the trip just a few kilometres outside of the city of Campbell River. The falls are most dramatic in the winter, when the river becomes swollen from the fall and winter rains and plunges over the rock face into a steep canyon. The newly built suspension bridge and viewing platforms make for a perfect photo opportunity of Elk Falls from multiple angles.

A year-round attraction, the 1,087-hectare Elk Falls Provincial Park has a lot to explore in addition to the falls. Although much of the forest is secondary growth, it is also home to the only significant stand of old-growth Douglas-fir north of MacMillan Provincial Park. The Millennium Trail, which connects the Elk Falls Trail to the Canyon View Trail, brings you through some of the oldest trees in the park. Near the midway point, a large gully of devil's club is worth stopping to admire, but stay on the trail and do not touch the large maple

leaf-shaped leaves, unless you want to learn first-hand how this plant got its name. Accidentally brushing the brittle spines that cover the plant is extremely unpleasant.

In the fall five species of salmon spawn in the park's waters. In the early spring, give yourself ample time to explore the Canyon View Trail on the hunt for wildflowers and birding opportunities. You may be lucky to find chocolate lilies, western trilliums and Pacific bleeding hearts, or the appropriately named western skunk cabbage. This water-loving plant will provide a familiar pungent olfactory clue as to its whereabouts. The skunk cabbage uses its distinct odour to attract beetles, flies and other insects, tricking them into pollinating its flower by fooling them into expecting a rotten meal. A beautiful, yellow bract, or modified leaf, surrounds a thick spike covered in a cluster of tiny flowers. Perhaps after taking some time to adjust to the smell, you will feel inclined to call these plants by their friendlier nickname — swamp lantern.

↑ The Campbell River plunges down Elk Falls into the chasm below.

↖ The western skunk cabbage is mostly known for its smell, despite its impressive beauty.

STRATHCONA PROVINCIAL PARK

Forbidden Plateau

The easternmost section of British Columbia's oldest provincial park is a must-do on Vancouver Island regardless of the season

What Makes This Hot Spot Hot?

- Unique plant and animal life dominates the landscape, thriving in both the wetlands and the difficult conditions of the alpine meadows.
- The Canada jays in Paradise Meadows are not shy, and visitors will find themselves surrounded by this bird during snack breaks on the trail.
- Views of Vancouver Island's mountains are stunning from Mount Albert Edward, one of the highest peaks on the island.

Address: Strathcona Provincial Park, Nordic Drive, Comox-Strathcona, BC
Tel.: (1-844) 435-9453
Website: www.env.gov.bc.ca/bcparks/explore/parkpgs/strath

GPS Coordinates
Latitude: 49.74525
Longitude: −125.31923

Open year-round

🚶 🔭 🎿 ⛺

♿ (Check ahead)

Canada jays are abundant in these hemlock forests.

In the heart of Vancouver Island lies the oldest provincial park in British Columbia. Established in 1911, Strathcona Provincial Park boasts over 250,000 hectares of dense forests, alpine peaks, glaciers and waterfalls. It can be difficult to know where to begin! Forbidden Plateau is one of the more easily reachable areas and hosts some of the most spectacular alpine landscapes in the park. Starting in the subalpine hemlock forest near Mount Washington's ski area, visitors can stroll along the Paradise Meadows Trail, where gentle boardwalks move through wetlands abuzz with dragonflies in the warmer months. In the meadows many unique and beautiful flowers bloom. Violets, monkeyflower and

mountain-heather thrive in the fields alongside the trails.

Hikers will have a hard time ignoring the Canada jays watching them closely during snack stops and lunch breaks. Although these sleek black, grey and white birds normally abide by the seasons by nesting in warmer months, a Canada jay has been seen incubating her eggs during a snowstorm. To her credit that particular storm was unexpected and came late in the summer. Researchers are interested in studying the Canada jays of Paradise Meadows, as their behaviour is notably different from other birds of the same species. These bold birds form large social groups and are particularly altruistic to each other: some non-breeding birds have been observed feeding nestlings. Researchers believe that the western Canada jays such as those found here may actually be a different species from the more eastern jays.

Both Lake Helen Mackenzie and Circlet Lake are fantastic backcountry camping sites. Lake Helen Mackenzie is an

easy overnight destination and a relatively level hike from Paradise Meadows. Circlet Lake, which sits in a natural basin and is surrounded by small trees, rests at the foot of a steep incline in the trail along which hikers can continue to Mount Albert Edward, the sixth-highest peak on Vancouver Island. At the peak, hikers are treated to captivating views of the surrounding mountains. Forbidden Plateau is a small but rich slice of paradise that is an excellent gateway to the rest of the park, where there is even more to explore.

⬉ Lake Helen Mackenzie features backcountry campsites.

↑ A series of trails and boardwalks meanders through meadows and wetlands surrounded by hemlock forests.

Francis Point Provincial Park

Fragile reindeer lichen blankets the steep banks of this Sunshine Coast hot spot

What Makes This Hot Spot Hot?

- A healthy population of reindeer lichen thrives along the rocky bluffs.
- There are amazing views of the Salish Sea, with ample opportunities for birding from the shore.
- The bluffs are home to rare species of plants and a high diversity of encrusting lichens, mosses and liverworts.

Address: Merrill Road, Madeira Park, BC
Tel.: N/A
Website: sunshine-coast-trails.com/francis-point.html

GPS Coordinates
Latitude: 49.61296
Longitude: −124.05919

Open year-round

→ **Giant arbutus trees thrive along these coastal bluffs.**

Francis Point Provincial Park protects a unique and fascinating ecosystem. The dry, low-elevation forest type found here occurs only on the eastern side of Vancouver Island and in limited locations along the Sunshine Coast, making this rare, protected hot spot a must-see. The park's main trail splits into two: the trail forking to the right provides a short walk up some stairs to views of the Salish Sea, while the trail to the left provides an hour's worth of hiking along the gorgeous bluffs.

If you continue on the left trail past the small lighthouse, you will reach a grove of giant arbutus trees. Their divided trunks sprawl out across the rocky edge and grow nearly horizontal to the ground before eventually turning towards the sky. The rocky bluffs are carpeted in a wonderful collection of grasses, wildflowers, mosses and lichens. The blue-listed dune bentgrass and a rare native subspecies of red fescue are present in this rich community.

The most prominent feature of the rocks, reindeer lichen covers large sections of the dry, wind-battered cliffs, adorning the landscape in a beautiful pale-green hue.

Lichens may be plant-like in some ways, but they are not plants. They are, in fact, made up of two or three organisms that are fused together in a symbiotic relationship: a multicellular fungus as well as an algae or a photosynthesizing bacteria, and at times a yeast, working together to create their own food. This pale, blanketing lichen only grows several millimetres a year and is sensitive to disturbance. It can take decades to grow and re-establish, so stay on the trail to keep this rare ecosystem intact. Adjacent to the provincial parkland there is an additional 17 hectares of protected shoreline as part of an ecological reserve. This area is not open to the public to fully protect its delicate ecological system, which has some of the densest concentrations of reindeer lichen.

Although the park is accessed through a residential area and can be tricky to find because of poor wayfinding, it is well worth the journey. The park is perfect for captivating ocean views adjacent to unique and biodiverse coastal communities and is an especially fascinating hot spot for those with a penchant for looking at lichens.

↑ The delicate branching of reindeer lichen, although extremely fragile on contact, can withstand the harsh conditions of these rocky bluffs.

↖ Careful footing and good boots are required as the trail can be steep, with both smooth, slippery rocks and sections laden with roots. But the effort pays off in abundance.

Goldstream Provincial Park

An old-growth forest within easy reach of Victoria

What Makes This Hot Spot Hot?

- A large chum salmon run attracts many visitors to the area.
- Bald eagles descend on the river by the hundreds to feast on the exhausted salmon.
- Majestic 600-year-old redcedar and Douglas-fir are found in this picturesque temperate rainforest.

Address: 2930 Trans-Canada Hwy (Hwy 1), Victoria, BC
Tel.: (250) 478-9414
Website: www.goldstreampark.com

GPS Coordinates
Latitude: 48.48475
Longitude: –123.54827

Open year-round

 (Check ahead)

↗ **Bigleaf maple line the trails through this old-growth forest.**

Towering 600-year-old giants in the form of Douglas-fir and western redcedar create dramatic scenes throughout Goldstream Provincial Park. Upon arrival, you are almost at once engulfed in a diverse and ancient forest, home to Western hemlock, bigleaf maple, black cottonwood and more.

Just a short, 16-kilometre trip from Victoria, this gorgeous park is one of the most reachable old-growth parks in British Columbia, making it one of the few places to experience an ancient old-growth temperate forest so close to an urban centre.

Goldstream is also home to a large chum salmon run, which numbers in the thousands each year. Observation platforms make it one of the most popular places for viewing this annual spectacle. For the adult salmon, this spawn is their last journey, and the dying fish draw in numerous other species that descend onto the river to take advantage of the easy meals. Hundreds of bald eagles visit the park in late fall and early winter to feast on the spent salmon carcasses along the shore, making this one of the highest concentrations of these remarkable raptors in the entire country.

Unlike most other species of Pacific salmon, chum are poor

jumpers and are therefore relegated to spawning in streams and rivers not impeded by waterfalls or human-made barriers. As a result, chum are more affected by habitat damage than are other salmon species, favouring streams hugging the coastal waters. Chum are the most widely distributed of the coastal salmon. They can be identified by the dark vertical bars, called watermarks, which develop along their sides when they reach maturity and prior to migrating from the ocean to streams and rivers for spawning. Sometimes referred to as dog salmon, the mature males develop canine-like teeth, used to battle for access to females. The best spawning sites are in cool, shallow waters, and the best time for viewing the spawning in Goldstream is from late October to the end of November, as chum are the last salmon species to spawn on the West Coast.

↑ The salmon are dying as they swim upstream to perform their final task, drawing a range of opportunistic predators ready for an easy meal.

↖ Goldstream Provincial Park is lovely in the late fall, which is also the best time to view the salmon spawning.

SATURNA ISLAND

Gulf Islands National Park Reserve

Saturna Island provides exquisite whale-watching opportunities — from the shore!

What Makes This Hot Spot Hot?

- Resident and transient orcas frequent the beautiful coastline of East Point.
- Unique oceanside rock formations provide additional explorations while soaking in the views.
- Harbour seals breed along the shores, and pups can be seen patiently waiting for their mothers to return.

Address: Narvaez Bay Road, Saturna, BC
Tel.: (250) 654-4000
Website: www.pc.gc.ca/en/pn-np/bc/gulf

GPS Coordinates
Latitude: 48.806687
Longitude: −123.165134

Open year-round

➢ **This large hollowed out rock is a great example of the Geoffrey formation rocks that overlook the shoreline.**

Easily accessible yet one of the least crowded of the Gulf Islands, Saturna is an optimal place for wildlife viewing. Nearly half of the island is protected as parkland, most of which is designated as part of the Gulf Islands National Park Reserve. This park covers 36 square kilometres spread over 15 islands, as well as numerous islets and marine zones. Within the boundaries of the park on Saturna, Echo Bay along the Narvaez Bay Trail provides beautiful views of Boundary Pass, the strait that runs along the boundary between Washington State and British Columbia, and looks out towards the San Juan Islands across the border.

The Gulf Islands National Park Reserve offers a great opportunity for exploring remarkable rock formations, best viewed along East Point where Geoffrey formation rocks dominate the landscape. The sandstone beds of the

shoreline erode in a pattern known as taphoni, or honeycomb weathering — one of the most distinctive features of this landscape. This type of weathering occurs when salt from the ocean crystalizes within the pores of the sandstone beds, prying apart the mineral grains and opening the rock up to other forms of weathering.

East Point is also one of the best lookouts in the province for whale watching from the land, as southern resident orca whales are regular visitors to the area from May until late autumn. It is not uncommon to see passing whales nearly hug the shoreline, and if you are really lucky, you may witness

fascinating orca behaviours as they socialize offshore: breaching, leaping or perhaps even spy-hopping, which is when they hold their heads above the waterline, becoming not only the watched but the watcher too. Transient orcas, which prefer to eat mammals, unlike the almost exclusively fish-eating residents, also pass through the area, likely interested in the number of harbour seals, as well as the Steller sea lions that visit the area in the fall and winter.

In the summer East Point becomes a special area for viewing harbour seals. Seal pups patiently wait on the shore for their mothers to return after feeding at sea. On average a pup weighs 11 kilograms at birth and quickly doubles its weight in the first month, feeding on its mother's rich milk. It is a delight to watch the young pups not only plod across the rocks in a caterpillar-like motion but also explore the surrounding water and become comfortable with the ocean they will call home. All visitors should keep a significant distance from any seals and pups while enjoying their playful antics.

↑ East Point is one of the best places in the province to watch orca whales from the shore.

↖ Echo Bay looks out across the marine border between Canada and the United States.

Helliwell Provincial Park

A beautiful nature escape on a lovely island, well worth the two ferry trips

What Makes This Hot Spot Hot?

- Dramatic, rounded bluffs punctuate the beautiful coastline.
- Old-growth Garry oak meadows are filled with wildflowers in the spring.
- Scuba divers may have a chance encounter with the elusive sixgill shark.

Address: Helliwell Road, Hornby Island, BC
Tel.: (250) 474-1336
Website: www.env.gov. bc.ca/bcparks/explore/parkpgs/helliwell

GPS Coordinates
Latitude: 49.51935
Longitude: −124.59811

Open year-round

↗ **This sixgill shark pup is a rare but remarkable sight.**

Two short ferry rides from Vancouver Island will get you to the shores of Hornby Island, a 29-square-kilometre island that includes an impressive expanse of protected wilderness. In the far northeast corner of the island you will find the ecologically diverse Helliwell Provincial Park. The park's impressive bluffs are distinct from most of the Gulf Islands, carved by glaciers that covered the island as recently as 14,000 years ago. As they receded, they left behind high, rounded bluffs and stranded angular boulders, or erratics, carried from distant locations.

The 7 kilometres of trails in the park weave through forests of old-growth Douglas-fir, Garry oak and arbutus trees, and out to meadows atop the dramatic bluffs. In the spring the shoreline meadows are covered with vibrant wildflowers, including the miniscule but charming poverty clover, a blue-listed species.

Lookouts of the rocky coastline give ample opportunity to watch for humpback whales, orcas, seals and winter congregations of sea-loving birds, like long-tailed ducks, white-winged scoters and common mergansers. Look out for black oystercatchers searching for mussels and limpets at low tide, and bald eagles roosting in standing dead trees as they watch over the meadows.

Of the 2,872 hectares of protected area, only 69 are land, while the rest includes the surrounding marine environment. Flora Islet, off the end of St. John's Point, was added to the protection of the park in part because of its unusual deep-sea visitors. Normally found up to 1,000 metres deep in the ocean, the rarely seen bluntnose sixgill shark has chosen this park as one of the few locations in the world where it visits shallower waters, attracting shark enthusiasts from all over the map. Most sharks have five gills, and there are only a few surviving members of this otherwise ancient family — some of the sixgill's closest relatives date back 200 million years. A sighting of these sharks is certainly not guaranteed, but for those lucky enough to see one, it will surely be a once in a lifetime experience.

↑ Glaciers that shaped the park left behind erratics — out-of-place boulders that dot the landscape.

Horne Lake Caves Provincial Park

An underground journey through geological history

What Makes This Hot Spot Hot?

- Water from melting glaciers dissolved thick layers of limestone, carving out the chambers and tunnels of these caves.
- Stalactites and other cave formations have been growing underground for thousands of years.
- Visitors can experience "absolute darkness." A true cave has at least one area where no light penetrates.

Address: 3905 Horne Lake Caves Road, Qualicum Beach, BC
Tel.: (250) 248-7829
Website: www.env.gov. bc.ca/bcparks/explore/ parkpgs/horne_lk

GPS Coordinates
Latitude: 49.34581
Longitude: −124.75095

Open year-round

Step into geological history beneath the surface of Vancouver Island. Over 1,000 caves make up a network of tunnels through polished limestone, giving the island the highest density of caves in North America. From Horne Lake follow signs through the forest on well-marked trails to two stunning examples of karst caves formed by glacial water dissolving the porous limestone. This limestone layer was formed during the Permian period and comprises millions of invertebrates that have been compressed into a rock layer.

The two self-guided caves are beautiful and well worth the trip on their own. Cave in groups of three to six, and be sure you have the necessary equipment, including two light sources per person, warm clothing and helmets. However, hiring a guide will provide a much more informative experience and give you access to some of the most spectacular caves in North America. Tight squeezes open into cavernous rooms, an underground waterfall seven storeys high cascades into even deeper passages, and in an area called the China Shop, large cave formations adorn the walls and cling

◂ **Visitors often stand in awe of the limestone cave formations.**

→ **A guide points out some of the interesting geological features in a cave.**

to the roof. Throughout the caves, among large stalactites, thin hollow tubes known as soda straws hang from the roof, taking upwards of 100 years to grow 1 centimetre.

Absolute darkness that results in a lack of plant life and a consistently cool year-round temperature make caves a hostile environment for life. The small number of animals that do live in caves tend to winter in them, or live near the entrances where they may leave to hunt. Keep an eye open for harvestmen, cave crickets and the long-toed salamander. Although bats are not normally seen in the caves of Horne Lake, they are present on Vancouver Island and sometimes winter in the island's caves. Wash your clothing between visiting any caving area to prevent potentially spreading the deadly white-nose fungus. While it is not harmful to humans it is quick to spread in bats and results in devastating population crashes.

MAQUINNA MARINE PROVINCIAL PARK

Hot Springs Cove

Geothermal hot springs meet the frigid waters of the Pacific Ocean in a coastal forest

What Makes This Hot Spot Hot?

- Hot springs cascade through rocky pools into the cool waters of the Pacific, making this natural paradise a literal hot spot.
- Local wildlife, a boardwalk through a cedar forest and oceanside pools offer a variety of sceneries and viewing opportunities all in one location.
- Visitors are given a unique view of British Columbia's rugged coast as they travel to and from the cove via float plane or boat.

Address: Maquinna Marine Provincial Park, Alberni-Clayoquot, BC
Tel.: (250) 474-1336
Website: www.env.gov.bc.ca/bcparks/explore/parkpgs/maquinna

GPS Coordinates
Latitude: 49.36689
Longitude: −126.27222

Open year-round

Remote, rugged and beautiful, Hot Springs Cove in Maquinna Marine Provincial Park is on many island-bound travellers' wish lists. From Tofino these natural hot springs are accessible exclusively by boat or float plane. Each offers its own unique and scenic tour of the wild west coast. Wildlife you may spot en route includes eagles, seals, bears and whales. The best chances of spotting grey and humpback whales is between March and October as they make their way north to feed in the cold waters of the Pacific Northwest.

Upon arrival an easy stroll along a boardwalk through a cedar forest leads visitors to a series of rocky pools into which hot water spills, gradually cooling before entering the ocean. Stand beneath a steaming waterfall before relaxing in one of the pools. The ebb and flow of the tide varies the temperature of the pools throughout the day, with the lowest-level pools being the coolest. After feeling the cold ocean water it may be difficult to believe that the Pacific Ocean is actually the source of the hot springs. Water from the Pacific moves through cracks in the ocean floor where it is heated before being pushed back to the surface. After completing a 5-kilometre journey underground, the water near the surface has a temperature of approximately 50 degrees Celsius. It cools quickly upon reaching the surface, but can be unbearably hot in some of the highest pools.

The springs are lovely year-round, and although spring and winter can be quite stormy, if you happen to be in the area on a nice day the off-season offers a more intimate experience.

Be sure to bring food, water and good shoes for the walk in, as well as shoes that can get wet while moving between the hot pools in the rocky intertidal zone.

↗ **A steaming waterfall between the pools.**

→ **Water flows between a series of pools into the ocean.**

↑ The boardwalk through the coastal rainforest is a great way to stretch your legs before relaxing in the springs.

Jáji7em and Kw'ulh Marine Park

Wildflowers blanket the delicate sand dunes of these small protected islands, which are only accessible at low tide

What Makes This Hot Spot Hot?

- This cluster of small islands becomes a wildflower haven in the spring and is only accessible by land at low tide.
- The walk out to the island provides perfect conditions for exploring the exposed intertidal life.
- The rare sand-verbena moth is found in the park thanks to the presence of its only host plant.

Address: Best accessed via a trail through Morning Beach Park, 7600 Denman Road, Denman Island, BC
Tel.: N/A
Website: www.env.gov.bc.ca/bcparks/explore/parkpgs/sandy_is

GPS Coordinates
Latitude: 49.61899
Longitude: −124.85222

Open year-round

Jáji7em and Kw'ulh (pronounced juh-jee-uhm and kwel) Marine Park includes a number of small islands called the Seal Islets. Sandy Island is the largest of the islands, with a stand of Douglas-fir at its centre that is surrounded by white sand beaches. This small, forested area is home to a bald eagle nest, and a number of other notable bird species make their way to this green patch, including Pacific slope flycatchers and Audubon's warblers.

These islands are accessible only by water or walking out at a low tide, so plan accordingly, including your return, otherwise it is a long wait for the waters to recede again! Low tide exposes a plethora of sand life: the seemingly limitless invertebrate specimens, both dead and alive, include moon snails, the introduced mudflat snails, clams, mussels, sand dollars, kelp and shore crabs, calcareous tube

worms, limpets and more.

There are also fantastic shorebird viewing opportunities along your low-tide walk, especially if you time your visit with the herring spawn in the early spring, when millions of washed-up eggs attract waves of wildlife to the area. Caspian terns and brant geese can be seen during their migration, and large numbers of dunlin and western sandpipers visit the area. Killdeer nest on the ground across the island, and you might be lucky enough to witness a protective parent feigning injury to draw you away from

the nest. Tread carefully, as their nests are nearly impossible to spot because of their impeccable camouflage.

Spring wildflowers are one of the main attractions of the marine park, and the park requires careful use of the trails, as this ecosystem is extremely fragile. The sandy dunes become covered in sheets of vibrant colours as the spring progresses — early flowers include goldstar, woodland star, blue-eyed Mary and red-flowering currant. As the weeks progress, clumps of sea blush, larkspur and chickweed begin to bloom.

This spectacular wildflower haven attracts some noteworthy insect life as well. The striking anise swallowtail visits the islands, and one special visitor has been spotted in this unique ecosystem. The rare sand-verbena moth is found in only four locations in all of British Columbia. Yellow sand-verbena, one of the 140 species of wildflower found in the park, is the only host plant for this rare moth, which depends on the plant for nearly all its life stages. Eggs are laid in the flowers, larvae feed on the leaves and the adult moths feed on the nectar.

↑ The land area of the park expands dramatically at low tide, exposing a whole new level of diversity in this hot spot.

↖ Blue-eyed Mary is a tiny but gorgeous flower found along the sandy edges in April.

↓ Goldstar is one of the earlier spring flowers to bloom on the sandy dunes of this marine park.

Little Qualicum Falls Provincial Park

Rugged rocks and a raging river are the main attractions of this beautiful provincial park

What Makes This Hot Spot Hot?

- This is an easily accessed park on central Vancouver Island, just off the highway.
- The upper and lower falls are viewable from trails and lookouts.
- Orchids can be found blooming in the spring.

Address: 4001 Alberni Hwy (Hwy 4), Qualicum Beach, BC
Tel.: (250) 474-1336
Website: www.env.gov.bc.ca/bcparks/explore/parkpgs/little_qualicum_falls

GPS Coordinates
Latitude: 49.3083
Longitude: −124.54241

Open year-round for day use but only May to September for camping

♿ (Check ahead)

Brilliant turquoise water rushes through the narrow canyons of Little Qualicum Falls Provincial Park, which is found off the Alberni Highway (Highway 4). Many of the cliffs are straight drops down to the water. Although strained and twisted trees grasp at the cliff rocks and soil to stop from toppling into the water, many have found their way into the torrents below, as evidenced by the large logs lying across the narrow gorges throughout the park.

The upper falls of the park have cut through rock, creating a tandem drop before the waters continue to spiral down the river in a hurried descent to the ocean, though not before crashing through another set of impressive falls. Bridges traverse the water to allow for views on either side of the river.

Keep your eyes out for the American dipper, a uniquely aquatic songbird that does not seem to mind the roar of the water as it bobs in and out of the torrents. These birds, with their nearly uniform grey plumage accented by their blinking white eyelids, walk along the river bottom searching for aquatic insects to eat. Dippers use the dramatic cliff faces for their nest sites, raising their broods high up on the rocks to escape predators and floods.

Winter and spring are the best times to view the falls because of the greater flow of water along the river. Planning your trip in the spring will also give you the added bonus of orchid blooms. There are many types of orchids along the forest trails surrounding the falls for those looking carefully. The calypso orchid, a single pale-purple flower with a delicate spotted lip, is rare across the province but locally common in this part of Vancouver Island. The western coralroot, another orchid, can develop up to

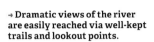 **Dramatic views of the river are easily reached via well-kept trails and lookout points.**

↘ **The nearly aquatic American dipper boldly feeds in the rushing river water.**

40 flowers on a single stalk shooting up from coral-like rhizomes. With no green photosynthesizing leaves, it instead saps its energy from fungi. In a complex and secretive underground waltz, fungi receive minerals and carbon symbiotically from tree roots and are themselves parasitized by the orchid.

PACIFIC RIM NATIONAL PARK RESERVE

Long Beach

This long, sandy beach may have you exploring the seashore for days

What Makes This Hot Spot Hot?

- Peering into tidal pools reveals sea stars, anemones and other interesting intertidal organisms.
- Migrating grey whales are frequently sighted in the spring on their way north from Mexico.
- Trails through the forest behind the beach offer interpretive signs and glimpses of the ocean between large trees.

Address: Pacific Rim National Park Reserve, 485 Wick Road, Ucluelet, BC
Tel.: (250) 726-4600
Website: www.longbeachmaps.com

GPS Coordinates
Latitude: 49.06758
Longitude: −125.74935

Open year-round

♿ (Check ahead)

➤ Surfers are a common sight amid the waves at Long Beach.

This long, sandy beach, spanning 16 kilometres along the west coast of Vancouver Island, is one of the earliest recorded surfing beaches in British Columbia. It is divided into three areas: Wikaninnish, Combers and Incinerator Rock. The seashore and surrounding forests offer many opportunities for exploration by naturalists.

From Combers Beach you can view Sea Lion Rock, a nesting haven for seabirds and a popular area for sea lions to hang out. If you are particularly interested in birds, loiter in the estuary at Combers Beach, where the river leaves the forest and enters the ocean. A mixture of salt and fresh water creates a nutrient-rich habitat, attracting birds. Trumpeter swans are known to frequent this area.

Migrating grey whales return from Mexico to the Pacific Northwest in the spring; stroll the beach in March for the best chance to see one. Other cetaceans you may spot include humpback whales, orcas and a variety of porpoises.

Hollows in rocky outcroppings create sanctuaries at low tide for sea stars, anemones and the occasional small fish. Safe from marine predators, these critters are trapped in these small tidal pools until the ocean rises again to cover them. Organisms that have adapted to live in tidal pools are unique and hardy. They must be able to survive a wide range of temperatures and adjust to lowered oxygen levels as the sun heats the water and animals in the pools produce waste.

On Wick Road, at the southern end of the beach, you will find the Kwisitis Visitor Centre. Interpretive displays provide information about the natural history of the area and the Nuu-chah-nulth First Nations. From here, access trails through the forest, which can provide a welcome respite from a hot day on the beach. You may see signs warning of dangerous riptides in the area, so swimming is not recommended in many places along this beach.

↑ Humpback whales are frequently sighted from shore and sea.

↓ Sea stars, like this ochre sea star, feed on barnacles and mussels.

MacMillan Provincial Park

While some trees remain standing, other fallen giants provide food and shelter for the diverse flora and fauna of Cathedral Grove

What Makes This Hot Spot Hot?

- Easily accessed trails wind through groves of giant trees.
- The park contains imposing 800-year-old Douglas-fir and western redcedar.
- Nurse logs provide nutrients and habitat for countless organisms.

Address: Alberni Hwy (Hwy 4), Port Alberni, BC
Tel.: (250) 474-1336
Website: www.env.gov. bc.ca/bcparks/explore/ parkpgs/macmillan

GPS Coordinates
Latitude: 49.2876
Longitude: −124.66648

Open year-round

♿ (Check ahead)

↗ **An entire community of mosses and lichens inhabits the trunks of these massive trees.**

MacMillan Provincial Park, often referred to by its formal name Cathedral Grove, may be the most famous old-growth forest in British Columbia, and for good reason. Douglas-fir and western redcedar, some over 800 years old, tower over their awestruck admirers. Most of the province's biggest stands of Douglas-fir of this maturity are difficult to access or, sadly, still being logged for timber, but this stand is thankfully very easy to reach. Despite its large number of annual visitors, this forest remains a treasure trove of natural wonders worth visiting.

In 1997 a severe windstorm swept through the park, and hundreds of these ancient trees fell. Although this storm impacted the trail system quite severely (some of the trails were never reopened), the ecosystem itself continues to thrive. The massive fallen trees maintain a vital role, even in their death. Sunlight, able to reach the forest floor once again, stimulates new growth in an understory that has been largely deprived of

→ Phenomenal giant Douglas-fir, up to 9 metres around, are protected within the boundaries of the park.

the sun's rays for hundreds of years. The stumps and logs of these fallen trees act as a nursery for new growth, providing nutrients and ideal conditions for the next generation of plants that sprout and take root on their decaying bodies. Nurse logs become home to a diverse assortment of fungi, mosses, insects and other flora and fauna, as the nutrients once locked in their massive trunks are freed up for other organisms to thrive on for decades to come.

Since the storm, the network of trails through the 301 hectares of ancient trees has been limited, but there is still much to see. On the south side of Alberni Highway, be sure to pay your respects to the largest Douglas-fir in the grove, which is an astounding 9 metres in circumference. On the north side of the highway you can explore a large tract of western redcedar near Cameron Lake. Do not forget your camera, as you will most certainly want to document your time spent among such noble giants.

Mitlenatch Island Nature Provincial Park

A tiny island with an impressive breeding bird population in the Strait of Georgia

What Makes This Hot Spot Hot?

- Thousands of glaucous-winged gulls nest inside the boundaries of this 155-hectare park.
- Other seabirds, including pigeon guillemots, pelagic cormorants and black oystercatchers, nest on the island.
- Harbour seals and California and Steller's sea lions haul up on the rocky shores.

Address: Mitlenatch Island, Strait of Georgia, BC
Tel.: N/A
Website: www.env.gov. bc.ca/bcparks/explore/ parkpgs/mitlenatch_is

GPS Coordinates
Latitude: 49.950757
Longitude: –125.002103

Open year-round

> A black oystercatcher is on the hunt for a meal.

Accessible only by water, Mitlenatch Island Nature Provincial Park, home to the second-largest seabird-nesting colony in the entire Strait of Georgia, protects a very sensitive eco-system. The trip to the island requires careful planning — several groups offer chartered tours to visit the colonies — but the effort to experience this extraordinary island first-hand is well worth it.

Although most of the island is closed to the public to protect the sensitive nature of the place, you will not have trouble finding superb bird-ing opportunities here. The park is seemingly overflowing with life, as massive breeding bird colonies return year after year. Thousands of pairs of glaucous-winged gulls nest on Mitlenatch Island. A bird blind provides a great opportunity for watching chicks interact-ing with their parents in June after they have hatched.

Pigeon guillemots breed on the island, their nests no more than a few chips of rocks or shells placed in crevices or under boulders or large pieces of driftwood. Seeing them come ashore is a special treat because it gives you an opportunity to admire their vibrant red feet.

The high-pitched repeat-ing "wheep" calls of the black oystercatchers become a familiar sound on the island,

as these birds nest along the rocky coast. Watch for them probing the shoreline for limpets, clams and oysters with their giant red bills. Pelagic cormorants can also be seen from the water, nesting right on the rocky cliffs. It is not exclusively marine bird species that nest on the island, though. Songbirds, northwestern crows and even a common raven pair have been seen nesting here.

In late April blooming wildflowers begin to blanket the island, including sea blush, chocolate lilies, common camas and even prickly pear cacti, which flower later in the summer. Garter snakes are often seen along the path that traverses the island. Watch for harbour seals, as well as both species of sea lion, California and Steller's, that like to drag themselves up on the rocky shores of the park. This area also becomes an important moulting site for harlequin ducks before moving on to their summer territories for breeding.

It is important that every visitor stays on the trail and respects the birds' comfort and space requirements so as not to disturb this island colony. Some species, like pelagic cormorants, are particularly sensitive to disturbance. Boaters and kayakers are asked to watch from a reasonable distance.

↑ Steller's sea lions are sometimes spotted up on the rocky shoreline.

↓ A pigeon guillemot shows off its vibrant mouth while calling.

SMALL INLET MARINE PROVINCIAL PARK

Newton Lake Trail

Take a dip in one of Quadra Island's many gorgeous lakes at the end of a rewarding hike through Western hemlock forest

What Makes This Hot Spot Hot?

- The trail leads to a great swimming spot on the beautiful, blue Newton Lake.
- This area has a wonderful representative Western hemlock forest.
- A wide range of bird and mammal species can be seen on the trail and around the lake's edge.

Address: Small Inlet Marine Provincial Park, Granite Bay Road, Quadra Island, BC
Tel.: N/A
Website: www.quadraisland.ca

GPS Coordinates
Latitude: 50.236856
Longitude: −125.290425

Open year-round

↗ **The clear blue waters of Newton Lake are picturesque.**

→ **Spirited red squirrels scold forest intruders.**

The Discovery Islands are a group of rugged, forested islands lodged between Vancouver Island and the Mainland, of which Quadra Island is one. Easily accessed by a 10-minute ferry ride from Campbell River, Quadra is home to some of the best lakes on the islands. Naturally, Quadra Island attracts many watersport enthusiasts, but there are abundant nature exploration opportunities by foot. The Newton Lake Trail is a great route for accessing these pleasant lakes without putting a paddle in the water.

Located on the northwest side of Quadra Island, the 287-hectare Small Inlet Marine Provincial Park is frequently used as an anchorage for long-distance boaters travelling along the coast to Alaska, but the park is also enjoyable when accessed from the land via a hiking trail from Granite Bay Road. Those looking for an even longer hike can continue past Newton Lake to eventually reach Small Inlet.

Although the start requires some surefootedness on jagged and uneven rocks, the trail eventually transitions to more manageable dirt and roots. Before arriving at Newton Lake, the trail passes a small marshy lake and through coastal Western hemlock forest. Western hemlock is one of the most shade tolerant trees of the Pacific coast. It also creates the densest canopy of all trees on the west coast, so understory growth is quite limited in these forests. As you travel along the gradually climbing trail, watch for Pacific banana slugs as they plod across the path looking for fallen leaves and other debris to eat. As the second-largest slug in the world, they should be hard to miss.

It is understandable why the cool, fresh waters of Newton Lake make for a popular swimming destination, especially after hiking a few kilometres on a sunny day. The lake reflects a deep green-blue hue, juxtaposed against lush green plant life that grows right to the water's edge. This swimming spot is a great place to look for red-breasted sapsuckers drilling holes in the bark of nearby trees. Sapsuckers

have a specialized tongue that enables them to soak up the sap as it flows from the holes it creates. Several species of hummingbirds take advantage of sapsucker feeding holes; for example, the rufous hummingbird has been seen following sapsuckers around during the day.

The best way to plan your hiking trip around Quadra Island is to pick up the detailed trail map published by the Quadra Island Trails Committee. This guide is available for purchase at various locations on Quadra, and proceeds from it support upkeep of Quadra's trails by local volunteers.

Oyster Bay Shoreline Regional Park

The mudflats of this small but lively park provide great opportunities for birding year-round

What Makes This Hot Spot Hot?

- Marine mudflats make this an ideal spot for shorebirds.
- Purple martins nest in boxes over the water.
- Large rafts of ducks overwinter in the protected waters.

Address: 1.4 km east of Iron River Road on South Island Hwy (Hwy 19A), Campbell River, BC
Tel.: N/A
Website: www.strathconard. ca/oyster-bay-shoreline- protection-park

GPS Coordinates
Latitude: 49.895213
Longitude: −125.147682

Open year-round

→ **Green-winged teals are among the many species of duck that take refuge in the calm waters.**

Despite its location right on the South Island Highway (Highway 19A), halfway between Courtenay and Campbell River, Oyster Bay Shoreline Regional Park is so small that if you are not looking carefully, you just might miss it. Even so, do not discount this birding hot spot, as the 4-hectare park features extensive mudflats that attract a mob of overwintering and migratory birds.

This area was originally created as a human-made causeway to protect floating timber that had been harvested from nearby forests, but natural materials accumulated along the shore after the log boom was no longer in use. The protected waters eventually developed extensive mudflats, now bursting with life. The smorgasbord of marine invertebrates present in the muck draws congregations of dunlins and black-bellied plovers in the winter. A little higher up the beach, among the stones and woody debris, you may see black turnstones poking around for a meal. Least and western sandpipers make stops here during their migrations to and from their winter homes to the south.

The nest boxes overlooking the flats become home to purple martins each spring, when you can watch their aerial dance above the water as they catch meals on the wing. The mudflats are not safe to walk on, but there is a rocky beach and raised dyke for observing the action along the shore. It helps to

visit the park outside of low tide so that the birds are forced in a bit closer to solid ground by the high waters.

The land barrier that once provided floating logs with protection from the rougher waters now attracts a large number of waterfowl for the same reason. At first glance, a large raft of ducks may look exclusively made up of mallards and American wigeons, but look closely and you may find green-winged teals, northern pintails and Eurasian wigeons. These dabbling ducks can be seen feeding almost continually by skimming the surface or tipping underwater to grab a meal in the shallow waters, spending a substantial portion of their time bottom-up. Although it may only take 15 minutes to walk the entire park, you may find yourself lingering a long while at Oyster Bay, as the furious feeding activity of the assembled birds provides endless entertainment.

⬆ Dunlins barely take the time to look up from their constant feasting on invertebrates in the mud.

⬉ A retired log boom in Oyster Bay has become a hot spot for bird activity.

PKOLS (Mount Douglas)

Four distinct habitat zones provide year-round nature viewing opportunities in this scenic lookout over Greater Victoria

What Makes This Hot Spot Hot?

- Early spring wildflowers add colour and even more intrigue to the rock outcroppings near the summit of PKOLS.
- The park offers impressive views of Victoria and the surrounding land and ocean.
- Four distinct habitat zones make this an important, biologically diverse urban park.

Address: Churchill Drive, Saanich, BC
Tel.: (250) 475-1775
Website: www.saanich.ca/EN/main/parks-recreation-culture/parks/parks-trails-amenities/signature-parks/mount-douglas-park.html

GPS Coordinates
Latitude: 48.49237
Longitude: –123.34543

Open year-round

 (Check ahead)

↗ **A cluster of chickweed monkeyflower provides a vibrant splash of yellow on the rocky slopes of PKOLS.**

With four distinct habitat zones, the great diversity of flora and fauna found within the 188 hectares of PKOLS provides endless opportunities for exploration and discovery.

Although still known to many by its colonial name, Mount Douglas, this biologically and culturally important landmark has been reclaimed as PKOLS (pronounced p'cawls), in recognition of its status as an important meeting place for many First Nations. Nation-to-Nation negotiations took place on the land, and this name change is a step in supporting ongoing efforts of Indigenous and settler populations to restore balanced relationships to the lands they call home.

The park boundary includes a rich coastal zone, where a diversity of intertidal life is supported by the eelgrass and kelp. The lower forests are home to an array of tree species, as well as a restored salmon spawning channel in Douglas Creek. Although trails are accessed from the base of PKOLS and range from easy to difficult, a road also leads to the peak so that the rock outcropping

can be reached more easily.

The dry and exposed Garry oak upper zone of the park is the perfect area for botanizing, as wildflowers such as shooting stars, stonecrop and fawn lilies can be found flowering in the spring and tucked into crevasses among the gnarled Garry oak trees. One particularly spectacular early spring flower spread throughout this zone is chickweed monkeyflower. Named for the comical grinning face displayed on each brilliant yellow flower, this wildflower can be found in dense patches in shady cracks of the rocky slopes on PKOLS.

Large numbers of white fawn lilies also pop up seemingly out of nowhere in the early spring, blanketing the forest floor at lower elevations.

The trails within the park range from easy to strenuous, and you can spend hours traversing through the different habitats on the 25-kilometre trail system. With spectacular views of Victoria, as well as the surrounding land and ocean, PKOLS is a must-see nature hot spot of lower Vancouver Island. Pack for a picnic and plan to spend the day exploring the largest urban forest of the Saanich Peninsula.

⬆ **Visitors can enjoy the sprawling view of land and ocean from the top of PKOLS.**

Rathtrevor Beach Provincial Park

A vital stopover for brant geese en route to their high arctic breeding grounds

What Makes This Hot Spot Hot?

- Low tide exposes intertidal life nearly a kilometre from shore.
- Brant geese arrive in droves and stay to feast on fish eggs during the herring spawn.
- Sand dollars appear in large numbers at low tide.

Address: 1240 Rath Road, Parksville, BC
Tel.: (250) 474-1336
Website: www.env.gov. bc.ca/bcparks/explore/ parkpgs/rathtrevor

GPS Coordinates
Latitude: 49.31863
Longitude: −124.27083

Open year-round

🚶 👓 🚣 ⛺

♿ (Check ahead)

→ **Sand dollar tests can be found across the exposed sands at low tide.**

Parksville's Rathtrevor Beach Provincial Park has 5 kilometres of hiking trails through old-growth forest tracing the shoreline and facing stunning views of the Salish Sea. That is reason enough to visit. However, visiting this park at low tide when the ocean recedes nearly a kilometre from the shoreline is the main attraction of this environment, for both people and wildlife.

Nestled against the smooth stones, soft sand and occasional colonies of barnacles embedded onto rocks, sand dollars are abundant at low tide. Finding a living sand dollar is rare, since most of the visible ones are dead and range in colour from pale beige to a light-tan leather shade. Living sand dollars are blackish-purple in colour and almost velvety to the touch — they are covered in tiny spines that they use to pass food particles to the specialized hairs that carry the food the

rest of the way to the mouth. Once dead, the spines fall off their naked, rigid skeletons, known as tests, revealing a five-petal flower pattern on the upper side, which signals where the tube feet would have been on the living animal.

The only sand dollar species found on the BC coast is the eccentric sand dollar, which can occur in dense populations and ranges from sandy bays to more open coastal waters. These animals are quite fragile, so living specimens should be left alone and the shells of dead sand dollars should be left for future visitors to enjoy. Collecting specimens in provincial

parks is illegal, and shells will one day become a part of the soft sand that makes this beach so spectacular.

February through April is the ideal time to plan a trip to Rathtrevor to see the migrating brant geese. These geese make the journey from Baja California, working their way up the coast and stopping in bays and estuaries during their migration. Brants can be seen by the thousands during the Pacific herring spawn when they, as well as countless other species, feast on the herring eggs that are washed close to the shore. By May the geese continue their journey to their breeding grounds in the high arctic — no other geese nest as far north as the brants. While stopped over in Rathtrevor, the brants are particularly vulnerable because they need to rest and feed to complete the remainder of their migration north. During the brant season, pets are not allowed on the beach. This migration garners such attention and even has a festival named after it — for almost 30 years, the annual Brant Wildlife Festival has been celebrating geese and all things natural in the area. Events are held over multiple weeks attracting nature nuts of all ages to celebrate and share in this natural wonder.

↑ The brant geese of the Pacific Coast have much darker bellies than the Atlantic populations.

↖ The expansive shoreline of Rathtrevor Beach at low tide attracts many birds to feast on the exposed marine life.

Ruckle Provincial Park

A unique park built on a legacy of farming

What Makes This Hot Spot Hot?

- Visitors are given a rare chance to learn about wildlife and farm-life in the same location.
- Extensive trails weave through diverse ecological communities.
- Opportunities abound for marine mammal watching.

Address: Beaver Point Road, Salt Spring Island, BC
Tel.: (250) 539-2115
Website: www.env.gov. bc.ca/bcparks/explore/ parkpgs/ruckle

GPS Coordinates
Latitude: 48.78061
Longitude: −123.38593

Open year-round

One of the Gulf Islands' largest provincial parks emerged from a legacy of family farming on Salt Spring Island, which dates back to 1872. Today visitors can still experience parts of the rich farming history on their visit to Ruckle Provincial Park while exploring the extensive trail system that brings nature enthusiasts through Garry oak meadows, coastal forests and rocky shorelines. The park is open for exploration year-round, although it is best to wait to camp when full service is offered in the park from the spring through to the fall.

For more than a century, descendants of the Ruckle family have farmed on the island property, making it the oldest continually operating farm in the province. Although a portion of the land remains a private working farm, BC Parks now manages the 486 hectares that were donated by the Ruckle Family in the 1970s. Although some of the original farm structures are still standing, including the farmhouse, keep in mind that the farmland is private property and should be viewed from the designated trails and roads.

The juxtaposition of ecological communities and human development serves as an important reminder of the

→ **There are many stunning views from the shoreline.**

⤡ **The park is home to the uniquely beautiful arbutus, Canada's only native broadleaf evergreen tree.**

impact humans can have on the Gulf Islands. Livestock on the farm and heavy visitor use of some areas have contributed to the spread of invasive species such as carpet burweed and Scotch broom. Park staff and volunteers are working hard to limit the spread of some of these damaging species. A mixture of sensitive, undisturbed areas starkly contrast with those places that have been greatly transformed by human activity. An interesting mix of Douglasfir and arbutus trees creates a unique setting before the forest gives way to the twisted Garry oaks that inhabit the thin shoreline meadows.

A rich kelp forest offshore attracts many interesting visitors to watch out for along the 7 kilometres of park shoreline. A variety of birds, including double-crested cormorants and bald eagles, can be seen looking for a meal in this important fish-feeding area. River otters, seals and sea lions are often observed rolling through the waves, and orca whales frequent the Swanson Channel between Salt Spring and North Pender Island.

Salmon River Estuary Conservation Area

A north island estuary that is home to a large population of Roosevelt elk

What Makes This Hot Spot Hot?

- Large populations of Roosevelt elk frequent the area.
- All species of Pacific salmon are found here: sockeye, chinook, coho, pink, chum, steelhead trout and cutthroat trout.
- As part of the Pacific Flyway, this area is an important stopover for migratory birds.

Address: Salmon River Main Line, Sayward, BC
Tel.: (604) 924-9771
Website: www.fwcp.ca/restoring-wildlife-habitat-at-the-salmon-river-conservation-area

GPS Coordinates
Latitude: 50.36999
Longitude: −125.94135

Open year-round

Although estuaries only occupy a small fraction of coastal land area, a huge number of species depend on them for parts of their life cycles. Along an otherwise fairly rough and rugged northern coastline, the Salmon River Estuary Conservation Area provides a nutrient-rich feeding ground and much-needed habitat for a wide range of species, making this a noteworthy estuary on Vancouver Island.

Aptly named, this particular estuary provides important habitat to all species of Pacific salmon, but it is a critical habitat too for the northern pygmy owl, the northern goshawk and the marbled murrelet. The estuary is also part of the Pacific Flyway, an important migratory route for many bird species.

In addition to providing vital fish and bird habitat, the conservation area provides essential grazing space for Roosevelt elk. These elk migrate locally and can be seen most often during the winter months when large numbers of them move down to lower elevations to graze.

There are about 3,200 Roosevelt elk in British Columbia, with over 3,000 residing on Vancouver Island. Their population on the Mainland has dwindled because of human development and activity, but the island remains a stronghold for this species. Populations reach their highest density north of Campbell River, but without extensive protected areas, these animals are forced to graze dangerously close to roads and human settlements. The largest of the elk family, Roosevelt elk play a valuable role in the ecosystem because they promote new growth by clearing underbrush through grazing. They are also an important food source of the rare Vancouver Island wolf.

While birding and botanizing along Kelly's Trail, also

↑ The Estuary Trail is only 600 metres long but provides lovely views of snow-capped mountains and shallow waters where the Johnstone Strait meets the Salmon River.

→ The calm waters of the estuary set the scene for perfect birding conditions.

look for places elk have left their mark in the forest — you might spot signs of antlers being rubbed on trees during the fall rut. Along the Estuary Trail, be sure to check out the bird blind that was installed for viewing the congregations of birds that feed within the estuary.

CAPE SCOTT PROVINCIAL PARK

San Josef Bay

The sea stacks of San Josef Bay are a must-see along the northern shores of Vancouver Island

What Makes This Hot Spot Hot?

- Sea stacks, weathered away by wave action, are an iconic image of the North Coast.
- The intertidal life is teeming with activity at low tide.
- Several beaches, including some with caves, are open for exploration during low tide.

Address: Cape Scott Provincial Park, Cape Scott Park Road, 64 km west of Port Hardy, BC
Tel.: (1-844) 435-9453
Website: www.capescottpark.com

GPS Coordinates
Latitude: 50.68498
Longitude: −128.26271

Open year-round

↗ The soft sand beaches, rocky outcroppings and waves crashing in the distance provide the perfect backdrop to your exploration of the North Coast.

Cape Scott Provincial Park is famously home to the North Coast Trail, a rugged and challenging weeklong backpacking trail. However, within the park there are also multiple day-use trails that allow visitors to experience this incredible park, on the most northern tip of Vancouver Island, without the challenges and commitment of a multiday journey.

The San Josef Bay Trail is an easy but rewarding hike within the park. After a 45-minute flat walk through gorgeous old-growth coastal temperate rainforest, the trail opens up to a set of spectacular fine sand beaches along BC's most western coastland. Plan your trip to arrive at the beach at low tide to explore the exposed tidal ponds, which are packed with chitons, anemones, huge snail colonies, sea stars, sand dollars and more.

At low tide, with dramatic, crashing open-ocean waves as the backdrop, the most famous and unique scenes of this park are revealed — sea stacks, which are towering volcanic

rock structures formed as the rough oceans wore away the rock, create one of the most picturesque scenes anywhere on the island. The stacks are topped with twisted and wind-battered bonsai-like trees. As you explore the beaches, there are opportunities to dip into sea caves and to view wildlife. Eagles, ospreys, scoters, otters and whales may be visible along the shore, and occasionally wolves visit these beaches.

This trip requires careful planning, as the logging roads to the park are heavily used and very rough — a truck is highly recommended. The weather can be unpredictable on the coast, and tide table knowledge is essential to make the most of this hot spot. That said, the planning effort is well worth it to visit one of the most beautiful locations in the province.

↑ **Sea stacks at low tide.**

→ **A breeding congregation of wrinkled dogwinkle can be found at low tide, with a chiton thrown in for good measure.**

Sargeant Bay Provincial Park

Shorelines, wetlands and a salmon creek to explore, as well as views of a rare peat bog at the end of a fabulous forest hike

What Makes This Hot Spot Hot?

- The deceptively named Triangle Lake is actually an important peat bog.
- A fish ladder was installed to support the salmon population of Colvin Creek.
- A beaver dam and lodge can be found in the wetland area near the beach.

Address: Redrooffs Road, Halfmoon Bay, BC
Tel.: (604) 885-3714
Websites: www.env.gov.bc.ca/bcparks/explore/parkpgs/sargeant, www.sargbay.ca/index.html

GPS Coordinates:
Latitude: 49.48001
Longitude: −123.86881

Open year-round

♿ (Check ahead)

↗ **The cheekily named fairy barf lichen can be found in Sargeant Bay Provincial Park.**

Although Sargeant Bay Provincial Park is only 57 hectares, within its boundaries there are many significant and varied habitats for nature lovers to see and enjoy. A pristine peat bog in a lush forest, beach access along the terminus of a salmon-bearing creek, a beaver lodge and a wetland separated from the beach by a raised bank are all ready to explore through a diverse trail system.

The 2.5-kilometre Triangle Lake Trail provides scenic views of old-growth forest mixed with largely coniferous second-growth forest and arbutus trees standing along rocky ridges, before arriving at Triangle Lake and looping back down to Colvin Creek. Upon arrival, you may notice this lake is not a lake at all, but a vital peat bog wetland.

Peat is an accumulation of dead organic matter, largely made up of sphagnum mosses. Requiring a narrow range of conditions to form, peat bogs cover only a small percentage of the world's land surface and yet perform necessary water filtration services for large bodies of fresh water. Unfortunately, peat bogs are becoming rare because of environmental degradation. A select community of plants are commonly found in bog systems, including sphagnum moss, bog cranberry and carnivorous plants, like the round-leaved sundew. The trail provides views of the bog, but the sensitive environment itself is inaccessible, since it is almost entirely

surrounded by rocky ridges. In the spring and summer you may be lucky enough to hear the calls or spot some activity of olive-sided flycatchers and common yellowthroats, two bird species that visit the bog in the warmer seasons.

The shoreline marsh provides great birding opportunities, whose residents include Virginia rails, great blue herons and many species of woodpecker and owl. Spring and summer mark the return of many migrant species, including western tanagers, back-headed grosbeaks and a wide range of warblers and flycatchers. A fish ladder was installed to allow chum and coho salmon passage to Colvin Creek from the ocean. Although industrious beavers have dammed up the waterway in front of this structure, a small channel, wide enough to allow the salmon through, remains open.

↗ **The moss-covered forest floor along the Triangle Lake Trail.**

↦ **Views of the peat bog from high above.**

PACIFIC RIM NATIONAL PARK RESERVE

Shorepine Bog Trail

A nutrient-depleted ecosystem home to carnivorous herbs and twisted trees

What Makes This Hot Spot Hot?

- Visitors can discover fascinating acid-thriving bog plants.
- Stunted trees create a dreamy, bizarre landscape.
- A boardwalk loop keeps feet dry and protects delicate plants.

Address: Pacific Rim National Park Reserve, Wick Road, Ucluelet, BC
Tel.: (250) 726-3500
Website: www.tofinohiking. com/hikes/bog-trail

GPS Coordinates
Latitude: 49.01354
Longitude: –125.65518

Open year-round

♿ **(Check ahead)**

↗ **A close-up of the sticky secretions of the round-leaved sundew, a fabulous carnivorous bog plant.**

Surrounded almost entirely by temperate rainforest, oddly gnarled trees help the Shorepine Bog Trail stand out as a unique nature hot spot in the Pacific Rim National Park Reserve. The shore pine, or lodgepole pine, found in this bog are stunted and mangled because of harsh growing conditions created by the acidic soils of the bog. Bogs are characterized by poor drainage and the presence of a thick carpet of sphagnum moss. The sphagnum acidifies the bog, resulting in slow rates of decay and extremely low nutrient availability. The effects on plant life are evident in the twisted and stunted appearance of the shore pines.

Plants have also evolved amazing strategies to thrive in these nutrient-poor environments. While some species found along the trail, like Labrador tea, bog blueberry, bog-laurel, goldthread and bog cranberry, depend on their roots to extract scarce but necessary nutrients, others have found a different means

of obtaining what they need — not through their roots, but their leaves. Round-leaved sundews are carnivorous plants with specialized leaves covered in tiny hairs, tipped with sticky fluid. This sweet-smelling fluid attracts and then ensnares any insects that make the mistake of landing. The leaves secrete enzymes to digest their prey, and essential nitrogen and other nutrients are absorbed to support the plant's growth. Although hawks, snakes and the occasional bear may visit the bog, the tiny sundew is a likely candidate for the most abundant carnivore in the area.

This 800-metre loop is mostly boardwalk to protect the delicate bog ecosystem, so please stay on the trail. The sphagnum moss in this area may be over a metre thick and hundreds of years old. There are plenty of opportunities for botanizing in this beautiful and unique pocket that should not be passed up as you adventure through the rainforests and beaches of the Pacific Rim National Park Reserve.

↑ Gnarled shore pine trees grow up out of the carpet of moss.

↓ A thick layer of sphagnum moss acidifies the water and creates unique growing conditions for other plants.

Skookumchuck Narrows Provincial Park

Nearly 800 billion litres of water crash and whirl through the narrows on a 3-metre tide

What Makes This Hot Spot Hot?

- The park has some of the world's largest tidal rapids, famous for their spectacular whirlpools.
- There is great tidal life viewing along the mudflats and rocky shoreline at low tide.
- Wildlife is abundant in the cold, nutrient-rich waters of the narrows.

Address: Egmont Road, Egmont, BC
Tel.: (604) 885-3714
Websites: www.env.gov.bc.ca/bcparks/explore/parkpgs/skook_narrows, www.skookumchucknarrows.ca

GPS Coordinates
Latitude: 49.73997
Longitude: –123.90915

Open year-round

Home to one of the world's fastest and largest tidal rapids, Skookumchuck Narrows Provincial Park provides an opportunity to witness an impressive force of nature, as well as enjoy some unique wildlife viewing opportunities in the same trip. As the dramatic turbulence of the rapids is completely dependent on the tides, be sure to plan your visit accordingly and aim to arrive for high tide to witness the peak power of the water.

Nearly 800 billion litres of water can be seen rushing through the narrows that connect the Sechelt and Jervis Inlets on a 3-metre tide, reaching speeds of up to 30 kilometres per hour. Turbulent rapids and whirlpools are created as tidal streams flowing from one end are restricted by the narrow channel, causing the tide to rise much more quickly on one side. This difference in tide depth creates river-like currents raging through the

area with each rise of the tides.

Watch for harbour seals and sea lions feeding and frolicking in the strong currents. Kayakers may also be seen flipping and rolling in the rapids, but please be aware of the fierce danger of these waters, as only extremely experienced whitewater kayakers should venture into the water as the tides surge. The dramatic flood tide can best be viewed from Roland Point, about 3.5 kilometres down the 4-kilometre trail. The North Point, just another 500 metres away, offers plenty of opportunities for viewing whirlpool activity in addition to wildlife watching.

Plan to give yourself enough time to also experience ebb tide in the park as the sea level falls, revealing rich intertidal life. Accessible rocky tidal pools are home to a wide variety of urchins, sea stars, crabs, anemones, chitons and more. The 123-hectare park is also home to many types

of waterfowl thanks to its cold, nutrient-rich waters. Overwintering grebes, loons, cormorants and other seafaring avian species arrive in the hundreds, including large numbers of the provincially threatened marbled murrelets. Bonaparte's gulls can sometimes be seen in the thousands.

↑ The rushing water creates whirlpools and whitewater across the inlet.

→ You may find purple sea stars at rest next to pink-tipped anemones in tidal pools.

Somenos Marsh Conservation Area

This urban wetland attracts some very large winter birds

What Makes This Hot Spot Hot?

- About 1,000 trumpeter swans call this wetland their winter home.
- An annual WildWings Festival celebrates the beauty and diversity of the area.
- Somenos Lake and Garry oak woods attract an even greater array of wildlife.

Address: Off of Island Hwy (Hwy 1), Duncan, BC
Tel.: (250) 732-0462
Website: www.somenosmarsh.com

GPS Coordinates
Latitude: 48.79179
Longitude: −123.70846

Open year-round

↗ **Pairs of tree swallows return each year to breed in the nest boxes placed around the marsh.**

Deemed a globally significant Important Bird Area by Bird Life International, the Somenos Marsh Conservation Area supports over 200 species of bird and is a worthy hot spot to visit any time of the year. Flood levels can rise over 2 metres in winter, turning fields into wetland. This is when you will see the most celebrated inhabitants of the marsh, the trumpeter swans. This marsh, situated along the Island Highway (Highway 1) just outside the city of Duncan, is remarkably the second-largest overwintering spot on Vancouver Island for these beautiful birds. About 1,000 swans may be seen in the marsh, representing 5 per cent of the world's population

of this species. As the largest native flying bird in Canada, they are a striking size, even for swans. With males weighing more than 11 kilograms, they need a lot of space for takeoff, which makes the fields of Somenos an ideal spot for the winter months before heading back north to breed.

The boardwalk and trails are kept in great condition by volunteers, and interpretive signs provide information about the local wildlife along the way. A little farther down the road, Drinkwater Dock overlooks Somenos Lake, home to waterfowl, songbirds and mammals year-round, including beavers and muskrats. The best winter viewing is along Watt's Walk when the fields are visited by many ducks, with greenwinged teals and wood ducks in good numbers. Two pairs of barn owls are known to

nest in the area as well. On the east side of the marsh is a Garry oak protected area.

Although tree swallows get their name from their habit of nesting in tree cavities, they happily raise their young in nest boxes. By the early spring these metallic-blue aerial acrobats will have already returned to stake their claim to the boxes around the marsh long before most other migrators arrive.

The Somenos Marsh Wildlife Society hosts an annual WildWings Nature and Arts Festival every fall to celebrate local biodiversity through guided walks, talks, movie screenings and more. This family-friendly event is spread over multiple days, and participating in some of the festivities is a great way to meet local wildlife experts and fellow nature enthusiasts.

↑ Summer in Somenos Marsh, before the fields surrounding the boardwalk become flooded with fall rains.

↑ Trumpeter swans become local celebrities during their winter stopover.

Sooke Potholes Provincial Park

Popular swimming holes transport you back in time to a period when glaciers dramatically shaped the land

What Makes This Hot Spot Hot?

- Salmon spawning occurs in the Sooke River.
- Glacial movement and meltwater carved the bedrock 15,000 years ago, creating dramatic potholes.
- Spring wildflowers bloom along the hiking trails that lead in and out of viewpoints along the river.

Address: Sooke River Road, Sooke, BC
Tel.: (250) 474-1336
Website: www.env.gov. bc.ca/bcparks/explore/ parkpgs/sooke_potholes

GPS Coordinates
Latitude: 48.42843
Longitude: −123.71239

Open year-round

⤢ **The nodding flowers of the white fawn lilies, one of the beautiful wildflowers in Sooke Potholes Provincial Park.**

Sooke Potholes Provincial Park takes you on a journey through time when these unique rock formations were initially formed, about 15,000 years ago. Envision the entire area covered in expansive ice packs, the massive glaciers scraping away at the surface of the land below. Huge boulders were carried great distances by these glaciers and deposited in new locations along the way. Beneath the glacial ice, meltwater surged, carving deep pathways through the rock below as it forced its way between ice and rock. The boulders left behind by the glaciers created additional weathering action as their motion and friction further carved the bedrock.

Today you can experience the spectacular results of an ice age long gone. Deep pools formed in river rock and the clear freshwater pools, reflecting green against the dramatic rock formations, not only are of geological interest but also make for great swimming holes. Note that in the early spring the high water runoff and surging Sooke River are too powerful for safe swimming, so wait for water levels to settle later in the year before taking a dip.

The deep canyons and the smooth, polished and sometimes very deep pools create a beautiful backdrop for nature viewing, as the area is also significant for its wildlife. Larger species, including black bears and Roosevelt elk, use this river as a corridor connecting larger spans of wild land. The river supports both chinook and coho salmon runs

as well, providing additional wildlife viewing opportunities. The Spring Salmon Place, or KWL-UCHUN Campground, is operated by the T'Sou-ke Nation. As this area is sacred land with an important and culturally significant salmon habitat, T'Sou-ke community members are helping to ensure the area and its wildlife are properly protected and respected.

You can see diverse types of wildflowers along the hiking trails that follow the river system. One of BC's most exquisite flowers, the white fawn lily is found in abundance in the early spring. These early blooming flowers are not to be missed, with their delicate nodding heads and the gorgeous chestnut-brown mottling on their leaves that hint at the flowers' association with a spotted deer fawn that is shrouded in the dappled light of the forest. These alluring plants live just a little inland from the riverside, preferring slightly drier and more open habitat to other understory flowers. The red-listed Sierra wood fern is also found in the park.

↑ **Dramatic rock formations filled with deep, green water are the major draw of the iconic Sooke Potholes landscape.**

→ **In the spring additional winter runoff transforms the green pools into dramatic, churning whitewater.**

Tofino Mudflats Wildlife Management Area

One of the most important wetland areas for migrating waterfowl and shorebirds in the province

What Makes This Hot Spot Hot?

- One of Vancouver Island's largest eelgrass beds supports a diverse aquatic community.
- Tens of thousands of ducks and geese overwinter in the sheltered waters within this wildlife management area.
- More than 100,000 western sandpipers visit the mudflats throughout the summer and fall.

Address: Main access via Sharp Road, 6 km north of the Pacific Rim National Park boundary, along the Pacific Rim Hwy (Hwy 4), Tofino, BC
Tel.: (1-877) 855-3222
Website: www.env.gov.bc.ca/fw/habitat/conservation-lands/wma/tofino_mudflats

GPS Coordinates
Latitude: 49.1023
Longitude: −125.85536

Open year-round

In addition to 338 hectares of forested land, this wildlife haven contains a staggering 1,770 hectares of tidal flats, eelgrass meadows, salt marshes and estuaries. As an integral part of the Clayoquot Sound UNESCO Biosphere Reserve, the Tofino Mudflats Wildlife Management Area is known as one of the most important habitats along the Pacific Flyway.

Where salty ocean waves meet fresh water from the surrounding land, nutrient-rich organic sediments are deposited, creating a muddy sludge that feeds a bountiful community of crabs, clams, ghost shrimp and ribbon worms. This in turn creates a nourishing banquet for travel-weary migrating shorebirds to feast upon. The mud can be nearly 2 metres deep!

The mudflats are also home to Vancouver Island's largest beds of eelgrass, a marine plant species that acts not only as a source of food for visiting avian species but also as a nursery for fish. These beds provide habitat for crustaceans and molluscs as well, which help feed the migratory bird populations.

The mudflats are teeming with birdlife, and not just during spring migration periods. Tens of thousands of ducks and geese overwinter here, and over 100,000 western sandpipers visit the mudflats throughout the summer and fall. In a single day, surveys have counted as many as 19,000. On top of the staggering number of western sandpipers, over 40 species of shorebird frequent the area, including dunlins, sanderlings, short- and long-billed dowitchers, black-bellied plover and least sandpipers. Throughout the year the area is a perfect location to watch for loons, herons, grebes, waterfowl and cormorants. The mudflats are also one of the 10 most critical habitats for overwintering waterfowl, including

↑ **A fling of western sandpipers takes off along the mudflats.**

green-winged teal, common mergansers, northern pintails, surf scoters, buffle-heads and mallards. The area draws in some of the highest densities of these birds in the whole province, which makes it a year-round birding destination.

The terrestrial lands protected within the area also host a great diversity of avian species, ranging from birds of prey to hummingbirds, that either pass through during migration or breed in the lands adjacent to the mudflats. Woodpeckers take advantage of the standing dead trees near the shoreline, and peregrine falcons are sometimes seen hunting along the mudflats during shorebird migration.

↑ **Semipalmated plovers follow a distinct behavioural pattern while feeding along the flats: run, stop, stare and snatch.**

PACIFIC RIM NATIONAL PARK RESERVE

West Coast Trail

A marine trail that is the ultimate adventure for lovers of the ocean and coastal forests

What Makes This Hot Spot Hot?

- Rich with history, this lifesaving trail travels through the traditional territories of three Nuu-chah-nulth First Nations.
- Visitors can hike through coastal rainforests and bogs and along seashores with tidal pools, all over the course of three to seven days.
- Whales and other marine mammals are frequently sighted from shore.

Address: Pacific Rim National Park Reserve, between Port Renfrew and Bamfield, BC
Tel.: (250) 762-4212
Website: www.pc.gc.ca/en/pn-np/bc/pacificrim/activ/activ6a

GPS Coordinates
Latitude: 48.57706
Longitude: −124.41772

Open from May to September

Tsusiat Falls is just one of the gorgeous beaches along the trail.

The West Coast Trail, 75 kilometres of breath-taking scenery, draws hikers from across North America. This nature hot spot is worth the preparation it takes to hike and camp for about five nights. The trail meanders in and out of old-growth forest, spending some time among towering cedars, and then moves to the rocky and sandy beaches.

As hikers pass by the old-growth cedar trees they may notice some have strips of bark missing. These trees are culturally modified, meaning the bark was stripped for cultural purposes, often strips would have been used by local First Nations for many types of weaving. Some of these large cedar trees were also cut and hollowed to create dugout canoes.

Having a tide table handy is necessary both for safety while hiking and so hikers can visit the beaches at low tide. On sandy or rocky beaches there is an abundance of inter-tidal treasures. It is no wonder low tide was referred to by various First Nations as "the table being set." Gooseneck

barnacles and mussels cling to rocks, and crabs scuttle about the sand. Search for tidal pools where anemones, bright purple sea urchins and a wide variety of sea stars and algae make their homes.

The views along the trail do not disappoint. One of the most picturesque campsites along the hike is near the stunning Tsusiat Falls, where fresh water cascades out of the forest and onto a beach. In addition to being beautiful, the West Coast Trail is rich in history. It runs through the traditional territories of three Nuu-chah-nulth Nations: Huu-ay-aht, Ditidaht and Pacheedaht. The rocky coastline was responsible for many shipwrecks in the 19th and 20th centuries, and so eventually lighthouses, telegraph wires and shelters for shipwreck victims were established along this trail, which at the time was named the Dominion Life Saving Trail.

The West Coast Trail is a through-hike going from Port Renfrew to Bamfield and does have a shuttle linking the two locations. It is well maintained by Parks Canada and requires a fee from hikers. Ladders, bridges and campsites are all in amazing condition.

↑ Gooseneck barnacles cling to the rocks in the intertidal zone.

↖ The hike is often along scenic rocky and sandy beaches.

Wild Pacific Trail

The vision of a man named Oyster Jim was put into action to create this series of free trails

What Makes This Hot Spot Hot?

- Hikers can explore the Ancient Cedars Trail to view towering redcedars up to 800 years old.
- There are opportunities for whale watching at the Amphitrite Lighthouse.
- Storm watchers frequent the Lighthouse Loop to watch powerful waves collide with the rocky shores.

Address: Ucluelet, BC
Tel.: N/A
Website:
www.wildpacifictrail.com

GPS Coordinates
Latitude: 48.93858
Longitude: −125.56079

Open year-round

The Amphitrite Lighthouse was built in response to a shipwreck that occurred in 1906.

The Wild Pacific Trail is composed of two main sections of trails that showcase the diversity of the West Coast. Along the trails, you can gaze out on the open ocean as waves crash onto the rocky shores and then admire an old-growth rainforest of cedars, some of which are hundreds of years old, towering over the shiny-leaved bushes of salal.

On the Lighthouse Loop, visitors can tour rocky shorelines en route to the Amphitrite Lighthouse. This well-kept trail with little elevation gain offers access to all.

Built over 100 years ago, the lighthouse is situated at the northern mouth of Barkley Sound. From here you can spot the Broken Group Islands and watch the sunset over the open ocean. On windy days, the waves wildly crash on the rocks, showcasing the power of the Pacific Ocean and making this a popular place for storm watchers. Search the horizon for waterspouts shooting out of the ocean or grey whales, humpbacks and orcas that could be swimming just below the surface.

The second section of the Wild Pacific Trail is a more

sheltered experience with a wider variety of trail options. Hiking the Ancient Cedars and Rocky Bluffs trails is a humbling experience. Giant redcedar, two of which are over 800 years old, tower above the trail alongside old-growth Sitka spruce and Western hemlock. Redcedars are sometimes referred to as the tree of life because they have so many uses to Coastal First Nations. Dugout canoes were carved from these trees, and redcedar bark was carefully stripped and woven into clothing and baskets. The Ancient Cedars Trail can be done as an independent loop or it can be connected to the Rocky Bluffs Trail, which follows along the seashore and provides visitors with views of beautiful rock formations and open ocean. Seals and sea lions are often sighted just offshore in a protected area known informally as the "sea lion pool."

In 1979 Oyster Jim Martin moved to Ucluelet to farm oysters. Inspired by his stunning surroundings, he soon thought up the idea of creating a hiking trail along Ucluelet's coastline. Eventually his dream was put into action. In 1999 the Wild Pacific Trail Society, which is responsible for the development and maintenance of the trail, was established, ensuring this incredible area would be preserved and freely accessible to visitors.

↑ Powerful waves and winds make it difficult for plants to survive on the rocky shores of the Lighthouse Loop.

↪ Cedar and fir trees tower over the trails, including the Lighthouse Loop.

Witty's Lagoon Regional Park

One of the most ecologically diverse parks in the region is worth planning a full day around

What Makes This Hot Spot Hot?

- Diverse habitats attract a wide range of species that thrive within the forest, marsh, lagoon and shorelines of this park.
- The picturesque Sitting Lady Falls is just a short hike from the parking lot.
- The park's forest is home to many bigleaf maples, whose giant vibrant green leaves provide a beautiful contrast against the conifers.

Address: 4115 Metchosin Road, Victoria, BC
Tel.: (250) 360-3000
Websites: www.wittyslagoon.com, www.crd.bc.ca/parks-recreation-culture/parks-trails/find-park-trail/wittys-lagoon

GPS Coordinates
Latitude: 48.38907
Longitude: −123.52461

Open year-round

→ **Flowering bigleaf maples along the forest trail.**

Although celebrated for its namesake body of water, Witty's Lagoon Regional Park also encompasses coniferous and mixed forests, sandy beaches, rugged shores and salt marshes, in addition to its brackish lagoon, all found within its 22.6-hectare area.

You will find many bigleaf maple trees amid the towering Douglas-fir along the park's trail, which splits and provides multiple angles to enjoy stunning views of Bilston Creek spilling over Sitting Lady Falls to feed fresh water into Witty's Lagoon. A dramatic cascade in the winter and early spring, the falls slow nearly to a trickle in the peak of summer. Although replenished with fresh water at this head, the lagoon is brackish thanks to the salt water at its mouth. The shallow and warm waters of the lagoon attract a variety of salt-tolerant animals that come to feed on the plentiful microscopic aquatic organisms. Migrating birds enjoy the brackish waters of the lagoon as part of their stopover in the spring and fall.

During the highest tides of the winter, the salt water floods over the spit into the

land beyond. Here the salty wetland conditions are home to a distinctive sampling of plants, since few species tolerate the salty conditions and seasonal flooding. The parasitic salt marsh dodders cling to the dense mats of glassworts in this unique site and are among the salt-tolerant plants that are a critical food source for visiting birds.

Time your visit right and you are in for a brilliant spring wildflower display throughout the understory of the forest. In Tower Point's open, grassy meadows you will find impressive numbers of vivid purple and blue Menzie's larkspur and common camas lilies.

The wide beach is often busy with visitors enjoying the sunshine, ocean waves and beautiful views, but despite being a popular area for human activity, there is still much other life to see along the vast expanse of shoreline. Hermit crabs scurry along in their hijacked snail shells, and shield limpets cling to their spot on the rocky outcroppings. River otters and harbour seals make the most of the rolling waves and kelp beds offshore.

↑ The winter runoff makes Sitting Lady Falls an impressive sight in the early spring.

↖ Common camas lilies bloom at Tower Point within the boundaries of the regional park.

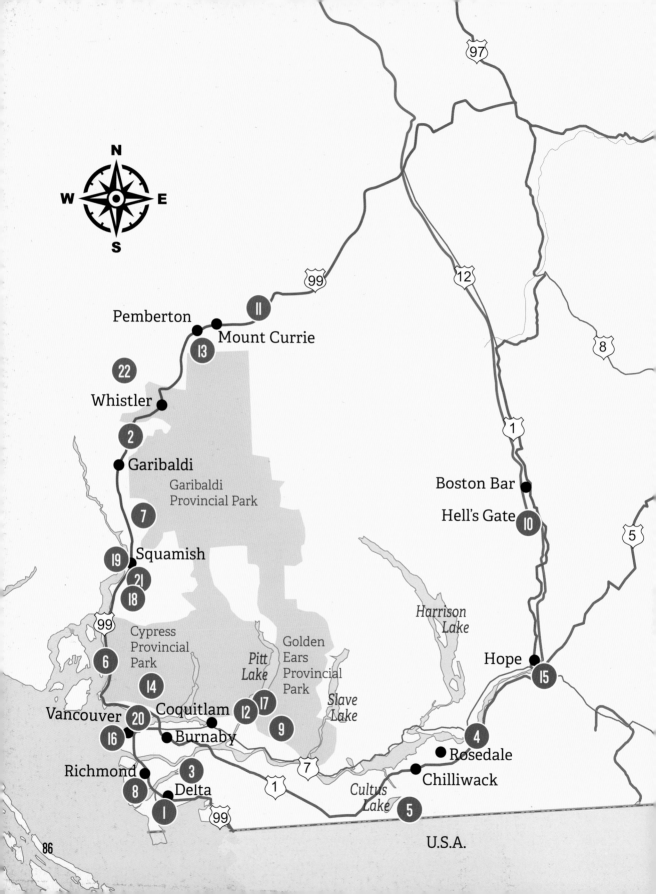

N
W E
S

97

99

Pemberton

Mount Currie

11

13

22

Whistler

2

Garibaldi

Garibaldi
Provincial Park

7

Squamish

19

21

18

99

Cypress
Provincial
Park

6

14

Vancouver

Coquitlam

20

12

17

Burnaby

9

16

Richmond

3

8

Delta

1

99

Pitt
Lake

Golden
Ears
Provincial
Park

Slave
Lake

Harrison
Lake

Boston Bar

Hell's Gate

10

12

1

8

5

Hope

15

4

Rosedale

Chilliwack

7

1

Cultus
Lake

5

U.S.A.

Lower Mainland

Boundary Bay Regional Park

This peninsula is vital to migratory birds and is an internationally recognized Important Bird Area

What Makes This Hot Spot Hot?

- Fresh water meets ocean mudflats creating naturalist opportunities for plant lovers, birders and the casual beach walker.
- Thousands of birds use this peninsula to rest and refuel during their migration.
- Birders delight in visiting the park any time of year as owls and other birds of prey overwinter here.

Address: Boundary Bay Road, Delta, BC
Tel.: (604) 224-5739
Website:
www.metrovancouver.
org/services/parks/parks-
greenways-reserves/
boundary-bay-regional-park

GPS Coordinates
Latitude: 49.01844
Longitude: −123.04974

Open year-round

♿ (Check ahead)

→ **The mudflats are a perfect habitat for marine invertebrates and attract many water birds.**

Boundary Bay is truly a birder's paradise. Be sure to bring your binoculars, as this park is an internationally recognized Important Bird Area. Thousands of birds stop here to rest and refuel on their migratory journey along the Pacific Flyway between Alaska and South America.

Over the course of a day on the beach you might spot a great horned owl perched near a trail, watch sandpipers feed in the mudflats, observe many different species of ducks and spy songbirds in the shrubs. These beach trails are set up for people who like to take their time and soak in their surroundings. The branching trail system has multiple viewing platforms with interpretive signs. Trails loop along the windswept shores, through forested and grassy areas and between salty marshes.

As the park sits within the boundaries of the Fraser River Estuary, fresh water flows into the ocean here, creating an environment in the mudflats that is perfect for marine invertebrates. This makes the park the ultimate feasting ground for hungry migratory birds. This varied landscape is also home to small rodents, which makes Boundary Bay an important place for birds of prey as well. The opportunity to view snowy owls and other birds overwintering here attracts birders during the winter months when the shores are less crowded. However, there is never a bad time to visit this park. May and June are particularly good times to view migratory birds.

The variety of ecosystems that supports all of this life also supports unique plants such as saltbush and salicornia, also known as sea asparagus, which grows exclusively in salt marshes and along beaches. Salicornia is a succulent plant that changes from green to red seasonally. If you look closely you may see moth caterpillars feeding on the plant.

As this is an important area for tired and hungry birds it is crucial that dogs remain on leashes and people stick to the designated paths in the park to allow the birds to refuel in peace.

BRANDYWINE FALLS PROVINCIAL PARK

Brandywine Falls

Rushing water flows from the forest into a cavernous basin surrounded by steep rock walls

What Makes This Hot Spot Hot?

- The forest is a protected area for red-legged frogs, a blue-listed species.
- Visitors get multiple viewpoints of the 70-metre waterfall carving its way through volcanic basalt rock.
- Dense pine forests, rare for coastal British Columbia, allow you to view a unique environment normally associated with the Interior.

Address: Brandywine Falls Provincial Park, Whistler, BC
Tel.: (604) 986-9371
Website: www.env.gov.bc.ca/bcparks/explore/parkpgs/brandywine_falls

GPS Coordinates
Latitude: 50.035992
Longitude: −123.119505

Open year-round

↗ **The northern red-legged frog may be seen in the wetlands around the falls.**

Whistler is known primarily as a skiing destination, but it is surrounded by natural beauty. Brandywine Falls Provincial Park is just south of Whistler and makes for a beautiful day trip. The falls can be reached on relatively easy trails that are a short distance from the parking lot. The Brandywine Creek exits the pine forest abruptly and cascades 70 metres into a large basin surrounded by steep, rocky cliffs. The surrounding lodgepole pine forest is rare for coastal British Columbia, an area that generally boasts moist cedar forests. You may feel like you are travelling through an

Interior forest, without the road trip. Glaciers shaped this landscape, wearing down the volcanic rock that the river and surrounding water bodies now occupy. With multiple viewing platforms a short distance from the trailhead, this waterfall is a stunning example of the beauty of British Columbia. Brandywine Falls is a spectacular sight in both summer and winter.

Snowshoers frequent the area during the winter months. Although the parking lot gate is not open during winter, a parking area alongside the road remains plowed. In the winter the basin is filled with snow and splash-back

from the waterfall freezes on the surrounding rock faces, leaving icicles hanging from rocky outcrops.

More trails in the park lead to lakes, streams and marshy areas. Combined with the forest this area creates a perfect habitat for the northern red-legged frog. A medium-sized frog named for its red underbelly and hind legs, the red-legged frog is a blue-listed species in British Columbia. Found only along the southern coast of the Mainland and throughout Vancouver Island, these frogs prefer damp forests with slow moving water. Keep an eye out for them on the meandering trails as they spend most of their adult lives hiding under forest debris, only returning to water to hunt and breed.

↑ **Brandywine Falls continues to carve the rocky landscape with a steady stream of flowing water.**

Burns Bog Delta Nature Reserve

The largest raised peat bog on North America's west coast

What Makes This Hot Spot Hot?

- The area is a key nesting habitat for the greater sandhill crane.
- It is home to regionally rare species, including Pacific water shrews, southern red-backed voles and painted turtles.
- Extensive peat bogs like this one act as carbon sinks, absorbing and storing large amounts of carbon.

Address: Nordel Court, Delta, BC
Tel.: (604) 572-0373
Website: www.burnsbog.org

GPS Coordinates
Latitude: 49.143545
Longitude: −122.929402

Open year-round

Burns Bog is the largest undeveloped urban land-mass in North America. At 3,000 hectares, its area is eight times that of Stanley Park, and it is a vital habitat in the Lower Mainland. Over 2,000 hectares are inaccessible to the public, protected as the Burns Bog Ecological Conservancy Area, but nature enthusiasts can still explore this special bog habitat by visiting the Delta Nature Reserve on the eastern perimeter of the bog. Raised boardwalks allow for great views of the bog and forest, but the area often floods, so come prepared for wet weather and a flooded walking path.

A vital stopover for migrating birds, the bog is an especially fabulous birding destination in the spring, but there are significant birding opportunities year-round. Burns Bog provides habitat for locally rare birds — blue-listed species found around the bog include purple martin, green herons, and barn and short-eared owls.

Keep your ears tuned for the bugling cry of the greater sandhill crane, which can be heard over 4 kilometres away. Most of the cranes pass through the area during migration, but the bog is also one of only a few nesting sites these graceful birds use in the Lower Mainland. Known for their dancing skills, sandhill cranes court each other using a fantastic display of leaping, bowing and flapping their outstretched wings while hopping and spinning.

The red-listed southern red-backed vole was once believed to be extirpated from Canada until a population was discovered in Burns Bog in 1999. The Pacific water shrew, one of the world's smallest diving mammals, is found nowhere else in Canada but southwestern British Columbia, and although in decline, this red-listed species calls Burns Bog home. BC's southwestern

population of painted turtles is also red-listed, so Burns Bog provides a critical habitat for the province's only native freshwater turtle.

This area is a wonderful spot for dragonfly enthusiasts, as it is home to species that are often difficult to find elsewhere in the Lower Mainland. Zigzag and subarctic darners are typically found in northern peatland habitat but can be spotted at Burns Bog, along with chalk-fronted corporals and yellow-legged meadowhawks.

The sphagnum moss in the bog began accumulating thousands of years ago. In some areas of the bog the peat deposits are over 20 metres deep. This is where the classification of raised peat bog comes from, as the peat is raised above the groundwater table. Peatland is an incredibly important carbon sink, storing vast quantities of biomass that might otherwise be converted into carbon dioxide and methane — both greenhouse gases. Peat is often used for agriculture, or extracted for fuel or horticultural use, so protecting peatland like Burns Bog is not only vital to the biodiversity it supports but also as a critical carbon repository on a warming planet.

↑ Raised boardwalks run through the nature reserve, allowing views of the bog and forest.

➡ A greater sandhill crane chick is a special sight at Burns Bog.

Cheam Lake Wetlands Regional Park

A restored lake and wetland habitat that was once drained for mining

What Makes This Hot Spot Hot?

- Over 185 bird species have been documented here.
- As many as 10 species of dragonfly and damselfly whiz around the park.
- Healthy habitats have been restored after water was drained for marl extraction.

Address: 53480 Elgey Road, Rosedale, BC
Tel.: (604) 702-5000
Website: www.fvrd.ca/EN/main/parks-recreation/parks-trails/cheam-lake-wetlands-regional-park.html

GPS Coordinates
Latitude: 49.197110
Longitude: −121.750426

Open year-round

↗ **Cedar waxwings make their presence known with high trills as they descend on trees in the park.**

Despite undergoing over 100 years of active mining and logging, today Cheam Lake Wetlands Regional Park is a vibrant wetland habitat replete with diverse flora and fauna. Over 185 species of birds have been documented visiting the parkland, just outside of Chilliwack, making it a wonderful destination for birding. Before becoming the park present today, marl limestone was extracted from the lake bottom for use as a fertilizer from 1944 until 1988. Two years later the park was created to restore the natural wetland habitat.

Many species breed here as well, including marsh wrens, western wood-pewees, tree swallows, Bullock's orioles, yellow warblers, common yellowthroats and cedar waxwings. Keep your eyes peeled for redheads, grey catbirds and American redstarts in the area, who typically reside farther inland but visit the park.

Cedar waxwings are often heard before they are seen — not because they are particularly inconspicuous, but simply because they are constantly chattering! Waxwings call often as they fly from tree to tree in search of food, their high trills and whistles carrying through the air. Cedar waxwings look like they have been painted in watercolour, their feathers smoothly transitioning between grey, soft rusty brown and pale yellow, and intensely highlighted with lemon yellow, red and black.

Look for flocks of these elegant birds as they search for berries to gorge on or dragonflies and mayflies to grab on the wing as they flit across the water.

Birds are not the only animals to make a triumphant comeback in the area after years of disturbance. Notable mammal representation in the park includes North American beavers, muskrats and river otters. Even bobcats make a rare appearance.

Cheam Lake Wetlands Regional Park supports 10 species of dragonfly and damselfly, including the small but easily distinguishable and aptly named dot-tailed whiteface. Look for them at the edge of the boardwalk that takes you to an elevated platform for great views over the lake. They may briefly perch among the yellow pond-lilies at the lake's edge. The massive floating flowers of this aquatic perennial are bright yellow and impossible to miss. What you are actually seeing are the giant exaggerated sepals, not the petals at all — the true petals are hidden from view inside the thick, waxy yellow cup.

↑ The park is nestled in the beautiful rolling hills of the Fraser Valley.

↓ The thick, waxy floating flowers of the yellow pond-lily are widespread in the wetland.

CULTUS LAKE PROVINCIAL PARK

Cultus Lake

This beautiful lake and transitional forest are perfect for a family-friendly vacation

What Makes This Hot Spot Hot?

- In the transition zone between two forest types lies a large, warm lake surrounded by tree-covered mountains.
- Colourful dragonflies and damselflies swoop in and out of the forest and along the lakeshore.
- Birds and other wildlife call this forest home, and with trails and viewpoints it is a lovely space for hiking and wildlife watching.

Address: Cultus Lake Provincial Park, 4165 Columbia Valley Road, Cultus Lake, BC
Tel.: (604) 858-3334
Website: www.env.gov.bc.ca/bcparks/explore/parkpgs/cultus_lk

GPS Coordinates
Latitude: 49.03729
Longitude: –121.99199

Open year-round

♿ (Check ahead)

↗ **The eight-spotted skimmer is one of many dragonfly species you may see around the lake.**

Tucked in the foothills of the Cascade Mountains, Cultus Lake is surrounded by lush, forested hills. The trails and campsites are well maintained, and the provincial park is family friendly. The lake itself is perfect for swimming, and plenty of wildlife can be seen and heard on the lakeshore and in the surrounding forest. There are deer, coyotes and some of the park's 100 species of birds to see as well as a number of fish species, including the endangered Cultus Lake sockeye salmon. Cultus Lake is encircled by natural spaces through which wildlife travels. The surrounding forest, too, is a transitional area where the coastal Douglas-fir zone meets coastal Western hemlock. These two forests combine to create a unique niche for wildlife.

Near the lake you will find dragonflies and damselflies darting between the trees and along the lakeshore. Requiring oxygen-rich water with plenty of plant life, dragonflies indicate that an ecosystem is thriving. Look out for the male white-faced meadowhawk and the eight-spotted skimmer. If you have the opportunity to

↑ The lake is a very inviting swim spot.

see one of these fliers land, get up close and have a look at the spectacular colours and patterns on its body and wings. The meadowhawk has a white face contrasted with a brilliant red body, while the skimmer has stunning black and white bands along its wings.

Explore the forest on the Giant Douglas-fir Trail. As the name implies, the trail leads to a huge 800-year-old tree — truly an imposing sight. On the forest floor you will find the leaves of the broadleaf maple alongside cones of Douglas-fir and hemlock. Another must-do trail is Teapot Hill, which travels through a shaded, mossy forest alongside a stream and opens to a spectacular view of the lake. The lake was once a large basin, but was dammed by a landslide. According to oral histories of the Stó:lō First Nation, the basin had underground rivers that led to the ocean.

↑ The lake is a very inviting swim spot.

Cypress Provincial Park

Escape to a winter wonderland for an afternoon and be home in time for dinner

What Makes This Hot Spot Hot?

- A wintertime paradise less than an hour's drive from downtown Vancouver offers snowshoeing and cross-country and downhill skiing.
- Named for the cypress tree this old-growth forest shapes the subalpine landscape.
- Forests and meadows support a variety of wildlife, including the snowshoe hare and pileated woodpecker.

Address: Greater Vancouver, BC
Tel.: (604) 926-5612
Website: www.env.gov.
bc.ca/bcparks/explore/
parkpgs/cypress

GPS Coordinates
Latitude: 49.40574
Longitude: –123.21762

Open year-round

♿ (Check ahead)

Vancouverites are spoiled by the many green spaces within their city, so it is common for them to forget they are also surrounded by rugged wilderness. Cypress Provincial Park provides easy access to the Coast Mountains and is just a short drive from downtown.

From mid-November through March a thick blanket of snow covers the mountains. You can snowshoe up the Hollyburn Peak Trail, which takes you through an old-growth forest to an alpine peak with spectacular views of Vancouver and the surrounding mountains. This trail starts at the Nordic Area of Cypress Mountain Resort, where snowshoes can be rented at a reasonable rate. The forest itself is composed of mountain hemlock, white pine, amabilis fir and cypress trees that are up to 1,000 years old. Mountain hemlock create small sanctuaries for winter animals as their flexible branches bow to the ground under the weight of the snow. Around these trees there may be tracks of squirrels, pine

martens and snowshoe hares, which are named for their large feet that allow them to sit atop the snow. Snowshoe hares are difficult to see during the winter because they change colour seasonally from a greyish brown in the warmer months to white to match the snow. While the hare may be difficult to spot, you will see obvious tracks where it has hopped between tree wells. Canada jays are frequently sighted in the park and are not shy of humans.

In the spring, marshes, lakes and fields of berries emerge from under the snow. The Yew Lake Trail is a short interpretive walk through marshland, while the Four Lakes Loop offers a longer hike through a variety of ecosystems. Look for the pileated woodpecker drilling small holes in tree trunks in search of insects. For experienced hikers the Howe Sound Crest Trail, usually done as a two-night backpacking trip, traces an alpine ridge along rugged terrain and offers magnificent views of Howe Sound.

↑ Covered in snow the trees in Cypress Provincial Park give the feeling of a winter wonderland.

↓ Snowshoe hares are often seen hopping between trees.

← In winter the historic Hollyburn Lodge restaurant opens its doors and can be accessed only by cross-country skiing or snowshoeing.

GARIBALDI PROVINCIAL PARK

Elfin Lakes Trail

Alpine lakes act as mirrors for the coastal mountains in this tranquil environment that is perfect for wildlife watching

What Makes This Hot Spot Hot?

- Black bears forage in fields of berries and alpine flowers.
- The area has unique panoramic views of the coastal mountains.
- Ideal for wildlife and plant enthusiasts the Elfin Lakes Trail meanders through a variety of ecosystems, from coastal forests to an alpine ridge.

Address: Garibaldi Provincial Park, Garibaldi Park Road, Squamish, BC
Tel.: (1-800) 689-9025
Website: www.env.gov. bc.ca/bcparks/explore/ parkpgs/garibaldi

GPS Coordinates
Latitude: 49.7884
Longitude: −122.98844

Open year-round

↗ **Delicate pink mountain-heather grows along the trails.**

Elfin Lakes Trail in Garibaldi Provincial Park is well known by Vancouverites and Squamish locals for its rugged beauty. As the trail approaches the treeline of the dense coastal forest, visitors will find the Red Heather warming hut, used by backcountry skiers in the winter. In the summer months the hut is surrounded by fields of rolling hills filled with flowers and shrubs in front of a stunning backdrop of coastal mountains. A lucky hiker may spot a black bear feeding on berries in the meadows. In the spring, bears live at lower elevations. As the snow melts, however, they move up the mountains into fields that are rich with berries and filled with insects they can eat off the bottoms of overturned logs. It is in the fall that hikers are most likely to see these bears gorging themselves on berries. During this time of year black bears spend up to 20 hours a day eating in preparation for hibernation.

Beyond the Red Heather hut the trail continues to gain elevation and the vegetation becomes typical of an alpine ecosystem with delicate

flowers and plants, such as the heather for which the area is named. The final stretch of the trail meanders along a ridge, with sensational views of the surrounding mountains, including the Garibaldi massif, on either side of the ridge. At the end of the trail two serene alpine lakes with a panoramic view make the journey worth every step. On a still day these alpine lakes act as mirrors to the surrounding peaks and glaciers. Hikers can cool off with a swim in the upper lake; the lower lake is reserved for water collection by campers. To hike to the Elfin Lakes and back is 21 kilometres, and although many do this trail as a full-day trip, there are also backcountry camping opportunities.

↑ **The stunning alpine lakes reflect the surrounding peaks on a calm day.**

◂ **Bears make their way up the mountains to graze in the surrounding fields.**

George C. Reifel Bird Sanctuary

Each year lesser snow geese arrive at their winter home and blanket the sanctuary

What Makes This Hot Spot Hot?

- Tens of thousands of lesser snow geese spend the winter here.
- Northern saw-whet owls roost along the trails during the day.
- Migratory birds stop over in huge numbers every spring and fall.

Address: 5191 Robertson Road, Delta, BC
Tel.: (604) 946-6980
Website: www.reifelbirdsanctuary.com

GPS Coordinates
Latitude: 49.09845
Longitude: −123.17847

Open year-round

Each spring and fall, during migration, thousands of shorebirds take refuge in the 300 hectares of the George C. Reifel Bird Sanctuary. The marshes, fields and sloughs of the protected area are a year-round attraction for birders, and the sanctuary is considered one of the top 10 birding destinations in Canada. To avoid the crowds visiting this popular spot, try to plan your trip on a weekday. The blinds located at multiple spots around the marsh make for great viewing opportunities, and the raised dykes provide the perfect setting for an early morning stroll.

Although the spring and fall are assumed to be the most exciting times to visit the sanctuary, its most famous visitors appear in the winter, marking their own arrival with enthusiastic and sometimes deafening honks as they lay claim to the surrounding fields and wetlands. Tens of thousands of lesser snow geese descend on the sanctuary in the late fall after completing their lengthy journey from Russia's Wrangel Island high in the Arctic. Despite arriving by the thousands, these giant gangs of geese may sometimes be difficult to spot because they do not stay in one place for the entire winter. If you cannot find them while walking the trails through the sanctuary, check the fields and estuaries that surround the marsh, since early morning disturbances can shift the birds to new locations. Look out for groupings of geese that include several greyer individuals — this is likely a family unit who made the journey together. The grey birds are part of the summer's brood yet to fully transition into their snowy white plumage.

Roosting during the daylight hours after a night of hunting, one of the smallest members of the owl family is frequently found in the sanctuary in winter. The northern

➜ Lucky visitors to Reifel might encounter the catlike stare of the northern saw-whet owl.

↘ Wood ducks are commonly seen along the paths throughout the sanctuary.

↘ Lesser snow geese cover the sanctuary and surrounding fields in the winter.

saw-whet owl is an absolute delight to see, and thankfully it does visitors a favour by roosting close to eye-level along the sanctuary trails. This small, bark-coloured bird with its dramatic white angled brow and cat-like eyes may be found on lower branches of western redcedar and Douglas-fir, or well hidden in holly.

Be very careful not to disturb the owls, even though they may be roosting close to the trail — they are trying to avoid larger predators and conserve energy until the night. By pointing out their roosts, you might accidently bring their presence to the attention of nearby passerines who will be sure to harass them until they leave the area. These enchanting owls are seldom seen despite their extensive range, and saw-whets are not often found here in the fall, so visit from December to March for your best chance to see one of Canada's most endearing owls.

Golden Ears Provincial Park

This gigantic park blends outdoor recreation with wilderness preservation

What Makes This Hot Spot Hot?

- One of the largest provincial parks in British Columbia, it is part of a much larger green corridor and is home to a diverse population of wildlife.
- This area was the traditional hunting ground for the Coast Salish and Interior Salish First Nations.
- Marshes and forests in valleys and along mountain slopes ring with the songs of the many birds found throughout the park.

Address: Golden Ears Parkway, Maple Ridge, BC
Tel.: (604) 466-8325
Website: www.env.gov. bc.ca/bcparks/explore/ parkpgs/golden_ears

GPS Coordinates
Latitude: 49.2501
Longitude: −122.53807

Open year-round

🚶 📷 🚵 🛶 🏊 🛶 🍴 ⛺

♿ (Check ahead)

🔎 **Named for its distinctive colouring, the chestnut-backed chickadee is a common sight all year long.**

Just outside the town of Maple Ridge and an easy day trip from Vancouver, Golden Ears is one of the largest provincial parks in British Columbia. Initially it was part of Garibaldi Provincial Park, north of Squamish, but was separated in 1927. Named for two distinct peaks known as the Golden Ears, the park's 62,540 hectares provide outstanding recreational opportunities alongside protection of its natural spaces.

Alouette Lake is an excellent camping and swimming spot that attracts locals and visitors from around the province. With numerous beaches and access to many hiking trails, it is easy to see why this lake is so popular. Before becoming a recreational area, the Alouette Valley hosted one of the largest logging operations in the province. A fire in 1931 raged through the valley, and much of the area is now second-growth forest. Nearly 90 years after the fire, it is interesting to hike between the new- and old-growth areas.

After years of logging, the forest in the Alouette Valley has reclaimed the land for

an abundance of plants and animals. The wildlife is difficult to miss. Pine siskins and chestnut-backed chickadees sing along the trails, and belted kingfishers perch alongside bodies of water. Goats scale rocky cliffs along the alpine mountain, and beavers are known to have dams in the many waterways throughout the park. Northern flying squirrels live in the trees, though they are nocturnal and not easy to see.

The hiking trails are well maintained and offer views of picturesque waterfalls and gorgeous mountains, as well as strolls through both the new- and old-growth forests and access to alpine peaks. The terrain in this park is quite mountainous so be prepared for some real hiking.

To learn more about the park, consider attending one of the interpretive programs offered during the summer months.

↑ Strolls through lush forests lead to waterfalls and other beautiful sights.

↖ Alouette Lake is a popular destination for day trips and camping.

Hell's Gate

A bird's-eye view of one of the largest natural obstacles faced by salmon that spawn up the Fraser River

What Makes This Hot Spot Hot?

- A sudden narrowing of the Fraser River results in the deep and rapid waters of Hell's Gate.
- A rockslide in the gorge caused a plummet in fish populations, but with innovative engineering the number of fish travelling through has been increasing dramatically.
- An aerial tram offers a sweeping view of the spectacular gorge.

Address: 43111 Trans-Canada Hwy (Hwy 1), Boston Bar, BC
Tel.: (604) 867-9277
Website:
www.hellsgateairtram.com

GPS Coordinates
Latitude: 49.78327
Longitude: –121.44733

Open in the summer

 (Check ahead)

→ **The Hell's Gate aerial tram gives visitors a bird's-eye view of the Fraser River.**

Hell's Gate is a popular place for tourists to take an adrenaline-inducing aerial tram over the Fraser River to a quaint area with a suspension bridge, fisheries exhibit and restaurant. But this area boasts much more than just a thrilling tram ride. The sudden narrowing of the Fraser River below forces a huge volume of water between granite cliffs only 35 metres apart. As the spring melt brings more water to the Fraser, the water levels increase. They have been recorded as high as 30 metres — about the height of a 10-storey building! The water here is so treacherous that, after visiting the canyon, explorer Simon Fraser described the gorge as "a place where no human should venture, for surely these are the gates of Hell."

While the geology itself is amazing, the most impressive feature of this place is below the muddy waters. From July through October thousands of salmon battle against the river's powerful flow to reach their spawning grounds — an incredible undertaking for even the strongest fish. Historically exhausted salmon would rest where the water was less powerful, along the shore or in small eddies, which are slow-moving whirlpools created by geological features. The ease of catching the tired fish made Hell's Gate an ideal seasonal fishing ground for the Nlaka'pamux First Nations.

Millions of salmon used to pass through Hell's Gate annually to their upriver spawning grounds. A large rockslide in 1913 during the construction of the Canadian Pacific Railway created nearly impossible conditions for the salmon to navigate. Fishing was restricted, and a variety of attempts were made to restore the salmon's migration pathway. Today you can see fishways on both sides of the river that create a gradual rise through slower-moving water for the salmon to use. These engineering efforts have seen a significant increase in the number of fish returning to their spawning grounds.

Joffre Lakes Provincial Park

Alpine lakes are fed by a glacier that continues to shape the landscape

What Makes This Hot Spot Hot?

- Travelling through glacier-carved terrain reveals how the receding Matier Glacier continues to carve the landscape.
- Mountain birds, including the three-toed woodpecker, live in the forest surrounding the lakes.
- Visitors can stroll through picturesque forests of tall, thin trees that are characteristic of alpine regions.

Address: Duffey Lake Road, Mount Currie, BC
Tel.: (1-800) 689-9025
Website: www.env.gov.bc.ca/bcparks/explore/parkpgs/joffre_lks

GPS Coordinates
Latitude: 50.354
Longitude: −122.48923

Open year-round

↗ **The three-toed woodpecker, with its distinctive yellow cap, may be seen on trees around the lakes.**

→ **Upper Joffre Lake has a spectacular view of the Matier Glacier, from which it gets its silt-laden water.**

A recent addition to British Columbia's provincial parks, the Joffre Lakes have been known as a recreation site for decades by mountaineers, but only obtained park status in 1996. The first people recorded to reach the top of the iconic Matier and Joffre peaks did so in 1957. Since then the area has became a popular hiking area to view the jagged peaks and mountain wildlife. A naturalist with a keen eye will spot many mountain birds, including the Canada jay and American three-toed woodpecker, around the lakes.

The Matier Glacier melts and feeds silt-filled water into three alpine lakes, turning them a stunning turquoise. Lower Joffre Lake is an easy five-minute walk from the trailhead and has spectacular views of the surrounding mountains through a subalpine forest of tall, thin trees. In the winter, snow blankets the trees, weighing down their branches. A combination of wind, cold temperatures and heavy snow causes the trees to grow slowly and have shortened branches, giving them their "thin" appearance.

The trail gains elevation as it approaches Middle Joffre Lake, where the view gets even better. The trees become shorter, and thin soil gives way to talus slopes characteristic of a landscape carved by glaciers. The trail becomes even more rugged towards Upper Joffre Lake, passing by waterfalls with small creek crossings. The chirp of an American pika or a rock shifting beneath the hooves of a mountain goat may grab your attention as you move into the alpine zone. The tranquil wilderness surrounding Upper Joffre Lake, situated in a bowl below rugged mountains, is worth the effort of the hike.

The trailhead to the lakes can be quite busy, so plan to go early and be sure to check trail conditions ahead of time.

Minnekhada Regional Park

A peaceful nature sanctuary nestled right in the city of Coquitlam

What Makes This Hot Spot Hot?

- Townsend's big-eared bats are found in the park.
- Visitors have easy access to marsh and woodland to explore.
- A hike to High Knoll provides viewpoints of the river and surrounding mountains.

Address: 4455 Oliver Road, Coquitlam, BC
Tel.: (604) 520-6442
Website: www.metrovancouver. org/services/parks/parks-greenways-reserves/minnekhada-regional-park

GPS Coordinates
Latitude: 49.299988
Longitude: –122.708405

Open May to September

↗ **The carnivorous greater bladderwort traps unsuspecting prey in the wetlands.**

With opportunities to explore a variety of habitats while traversing just a few kilometres of walking trails, the easily accessed Minnekhada Regional Park is a great place to explore for the day with binoculars and bug net in hand. Hiking to the High Knoll viewpoint gives you great views over Pitt River and the surrounding area, with Mount Baker and the mountains of Golden Ears Provincial Park as the backdrop.

The park is home to many species of birds that reflect the diversity of habitats they can access within its boundaries. American bitterns, soras and Virginia rails lurk around the edges of the marshes, and there is a great deal of woodpeckers in the birch and alder stands, as well as among the evergreens in the older woodland. In the spring many types of swallows visit the marsh, including tree, violet-green and barn swallows. Even cliff and northern rough-winged swallows have been seen in the area. Waterfowl over-winter in the park, and it is one of the best places to spot ring-necked ducks in the area.

In the park's marsh, look for the yellow flowers of the greater bladderwort. These free-floating aquatic plants are carnivorous, using their tiny valve-lidded bladders not only for buoyancy but also to trap small crustaceans and other animals. The valves have stiff bristles that trigger the bladder to open and expand, and the resulting rush of water engulfs the unsuspecting animal inside the bladder.

Visit the park at dusk and you may be lucky enough to encounter one of its four species of bats, including

the vulnerable Townsend's big-eared bat. Appropriately named, the bats have ears that measure nearly half the length of their body. These bats do not hide in crevices while they roost like many other bats, which, combined with their preference for lower elevation areas, makes them particularly vulnerable to human disturbance. If you can, join in one of the park's evening bat interpretive programs to learn more about this special animal.

↑ **The picturesque marshes of this regional park are a must-see.**

← **The Townsend's big-eared bat calls this park home.**

Nairn Falls Provincial Park

Water cascades between water-carved potholes in the Green River

What Makes This Hot Spot Hot?

- British Columbia's provincial flower, the Pacific dogwood (a flowering tree), grows alongside a river coloured turquoise by glacial silt.
- Lucky hikers can catch a glimpse of the rubber boa, a well-camouflaged and harmless snake.
- Trails take hikers through tranquil coastal forests of cedar and hemlock.

Address: Sea-to-Sky Hwy (Hwy 99), 4 km south of Pemberton, BC
Tel.: (604) 986-9371
Website: www.env.gov. bc.ca/bcparks/explore/parkpgs/nairn_falls

GPS Coordinates
Latitude: 50.29352
Longitude: −122.82507

Open year-round; campground open May 12 to October 1

The Green River flows through the centre of Nairn Falls Provincial Park, which sits between Whistler and Pemberton. The rushing river is named for its turquoise colour resulting from sunlight reflecting off glacial silt. The beauty and location of the park make it a perfect place to set up camp while exploring this and other nature hot spots of the Sea-to-Sky Corridor. Although there are a few trails to hike within the park, the Nairn Falls Trail, which leads to the namesake waterfalls, is a must. The trail follows the Green River through coastal forests of cedar and hemlock for about half an hour before coming to upper and lower Nairn Falls.

The power of the water is evident by the smoothed granite through which the water has carved its path. The falls cascade over the rock and have created potholes where the water pools and churns, sending mist into the air, before falling farther. Rocky outcrops along the trail provide spectacular viewpoints of the falls. This trail was historically used by the Lil'wat Nation to gain access to Nairn Falls as well as to Mount Currie, the massive

picturesque peak towering over the valley. The trail is fairly easy but does have a couple steep drop-offs down to the river valley, so ensure you wear sturdy footwear.

Another notable hike in the park is the Coudre Point Trail, which meanders in and out of the forest along the river. In the park expect to see the Pacific dogwood, a flowering tree and British Columbia's provincial flower, along with deer and other wildlife. Also keep an eye out for the elusive rubber boa, which is the smallest member of the boa constrictor family. Completely harmless, these boas are greenish-brown and camouflage well on the forest floor. If one feels threatened it will curl into a small ball and poke its tail out. Their tail acts as a decoy to predators because it looks very similar to its head.

On hot summer days One Mile Lake, just north of the park closer to Pemberton, is an excellent place for a swim.

⬆ The stunning waters of the Green River have carved beautiful features in the rock over which it tumbles and flows.

⬉ The Pacific dogwood blossoms alongside the trail.

LYNN HEADWATERS REGIONAL PARK

Norvan Falls

Impressive falls are the highlight of a fungi-packed walk through North Vancouver wilderness

What Makes This Hot Spot Hot?

- Fall is a great time for a visit to experience the seasonal outburst of mushroom growth in the area.
- Accessible by public transit, this park is one of the most reachable hiking destinations in the region.
- Norvan Falls is a beautiful reward at the end of a hike that weaves along the water's edge through temperate forest.

Address: 4900 Lynn Valley Road, North Vancouver, BC
Tel.: (604) 224-5739
Website: www.metrovancouver.org/services/parks/parks-greenways-reserves/lynn-headwaters-regional-park

GPS Coordinates
Latitude: 49.36157
Longitude: −123.0281

Open year-round

♿ (Check ahead)

↗ **Mycology enthusiasts are not the only individuals to take advantage of the autumn eruption of fungal growth, as this banana slug makes quick work of its mushroom meal.**

Lynn Headwaters Regional Park is criss-crossed with trails of varying difficulty and elevation, but one of the easiest hikes in this substantial protected land is to Norvan Falls, which can be accessed year-round if the weather co-operates.

The first section of the trail is a wide path that largely hugs the edge of Lynn Creek, with many access points to pop in and explore the clear waters and large stones of the river's edge. Look out for remnants of early logging activity in the area, where tools long forgotten still lie, idle and rusted.

After veering off Lynn Loop Trail onto Headwaters Trail and continuing along for a few more kilometres, you will hear the unmistakable sound of Norvan Creek rushing over the falls, signalling that you have nearly reached your destination, although there are opportunities to continue farther into the park. A steep path allows you to make your way down towards the edge of the creek below the falls, providing impressive views and a great afternoon picnic location.

This hike through second-growth temperate forest drenched in moisture and moss is perfect for mycology enthusiasts to explore in the

→ The view from the base of Norvan Falls.

↘ Although it looks a bit like a toasted marshmallow, the Shaggy Scalycap is not one of BC's edible mushroom species.

fall. Most of this diverse set of fungal species becomes more noticeable when fruiting bodies spring forth from decaying organic matter in the autumn, especially along fallen logs and up the trunks of dead or dying trees. The visible part of each mushroom is only a small portion of the entire organism. Most of the year, fungi stay hidden from view, made up of hyphae, hairlike filaments that spread out and penetrate the decaying host. This network of hyphae, called the mycelium, forms a fruiting structure when it is ready to spread its spores.

One favourite mushroom to look out for is the wonderfully named Shaggy Scalycap, typically found near the base of trees and stumps. It brings to mind a vision of toasted marshmallows around the campfire. This charming inhabitant is just one of innumerable species of fungi worth searching for in the park — the shapes, sizes, colours and textures of the fungi here are well worth a journey into the forest during the fall rains.

COQUIHALLA CANYON PROVINCIAL PARK

Othello Tunnels

Historic tunnels offer access to a spectacular view of a water-carved gorge

What Makes This Hot Spot Hot?

- Visitors can explore the historic tunnels of the Kettle Valley Railway, which were carved through granite.
- The powerful waters of the Coquihalla River have sculpted a unique river canyon.
- Coastal forests composed of cedar, hemlock, Douglas-fir and maple make for a perfect stroll.

Address: Kettle Valley Trail, Coquihalla Canyon Provincial Park, Hope, BC
Tel.: (604) 869-2021
Website: www.env.gov. bc.ca/bcparks/explore/ parkpgs/coquihalla_cyn

GPS Coordinates
Latitude: 49.3778
Longitude: −121.36952

Open April 1 to October 31

🚶 🚲

♿ (Check ahead)

A historic site and a geological adventure, the Othello Tunnels are an important piece of Canadian history and offer visitors a unique perspective of granite bedrock. Named for the Shakespearean tragedy Othello, the series of five tunnels is part of the Kettle Valley Railway, which allowed trains to complete the cross-Canada journey.

As you stroll or bike along the path, now stripped of the railway, you will encounter interpretive signage about the history of the area. Over time the river has carved through approximately 300 vertical feet of granite, creating a picturesque gorge. The railway, completed in the early 1900s, passed through these granite walls and over the raging Coquihalla River below. Constructing the railway was no small feat considering the tools and technology available at the time. Many engineers suggested bypassing the gorge altogether. However, Andrew McCulloch, who became the chief engineer of the tunnels, saw the potential of building through the gorge. Using rope suspension bridges and hanging ladders, among other innovative techniques,

labourers completed a truly impressive task in a challenging canyon environment.

Today the tunnels offer a unique view of the river gorge. Observing river canyons such as this is generally reserved for experienced kayakers and whitewater paddlers. The tunnels make it possible to hike alongside the river and take in the majestic view of the vertical granite cliffs towering over the powerful whitewater that continues to erode the rocky riverbed. The area is not all moss-covered granite and steep drops. The trail travels through lush forests of hemlock, cedar, fir and maple, which continue along the riverbank as the water flows into the Fraser River. Black-throated grey warblers and varied thrushes are common sights in the forest surrounding the tunnels. The forest is also an excellent habitat for black-tailed deer.

Falling rocks and ice make it dangerous to visit the tunnels during the winter months, so be sure to comply with the opening times and check conditions ahead of visiting.

↑ A series of trestles and tunnels leads through a granite gorge.

↖ Black-tailed deer call the surrounding forest home.

Pacific Spirit Regional Park

A stunning natural space teeming with life right in the city of Vancouver

What Makes This Hot Spot Hot?

- A variety of ecosystems and easy access by public transit make this park a wilderness wonderland.
- Marsh, old-growth cedars, rocky intertidal zone and an abundance of wildlife are all within 20 minutes of hiking.
- Birds, squirrels and many other forest residents give the space a tranquil, wild feeling within the city.

Address: 5495 Chancellor Boulevard, Vancouver, BC (For more information about access points, see the park map on the website below.)
Tel.: (604) 224-5739
Website: www.metrovancouver.org/services/parks/parks-greenways-reserves/pacific-spirit-regional-park

GPS Coordinates
Latitude: 49.25307
Longitude: −123.21639

Open year-round

⚲ **Great horned owls and other birds are heard in the forest.**

Passing through a forest is part of the daily commute for many lucky university students. Pacific Spirit Regional Park, composed of rainforests, beaches, bogs and estuaries, covers 308 hectares with over 70 kilometres of trails. This green space sits between the University of British Columbia and the city of Vancouver. In the heart of an old-growth forest, standing beneath towering cedars and Douglas-fir, visitors feel surrounded by rugged wilderness — a true escape from the hustle and bustle of the city.

Native plants are abundant and diverse. Near the cedars are alders and vine maples looming over salmonberry bushes, as the waxy leaves of salal shine in among ferns and flowers. In an effort to protect this diverse area, which was originally part of the UBC's endowment land, the site was established as a regional park in 1989. It is now maintained by the dedicated volunteers of the Pacific Spirit Park Society and Metro Vancouver.

Different ecosystems are accessible from the park's many entrances. Crabs scurry through the intertidal zone at Acadia Beach, while sword ferns line a shaded path through the forest just a stone's throw away. Following a short loop from Acadia Beach along the Salish Trail, connecting to the Spanish Trail and ending at Spanish Banks Beach (all of which is just a small percentage of the park's trails), a hiker will encounter sandy and rocky beaches, go on a beautiful canyon-side stroll and explore wetlands next to an old-growth forest. Bird, amphibian and small mammal sightings are common. Pacific wrens and

small songbirds sing along the trails, great horned owls are often heard in the evenings hooting from tree branches above and bald eagles are a regular sight as they swoop down from trees to catch fish. Occasionally larger mammals, such as coyotes, are sighted. With all this plant and animal life, this park is truly one of the most accessible and diverse natural spaces in the province, and it is right in the heart of Vancouver.

⇡ Ferns and moss cover the understory of the park's lush treed areas.

⬉ The rocky intertidal zone hosts many marine invertebrates, such as barnacles, mussels and crabs.

Pitt-Addington Marsh Wildlife Management Area

Forty kilometres east of Vancouver, this wetland habitat is an important area for birds in the Lower Mainland

What Makes This Hot Spot Hot?

- The habitat is one of the only coastal breeding grounds of the grey catbird.
- Ninety species of songbirds have been recorded in the area.
- There are over 50 kilometres of raised dykes to explore between tracts of marshland.

Address: Rannie Road, Pitt Meadows, BC
Tel.: N/A
Website: www.env.gov.bc.ca/fw/habitat/conservation-lands/wma/pitt_addington

GPS Coordinates
Latitude: 49.329929
Longitude: −122.637629

Open year-round

→ **A perched blue dasher watches over his territory.**

The many kilometres of dykes and trails that traverse the Pitt-Addington Marsh Wildlife Management Area allow for countless hours of birding year-round. Over 50 kilometres of accessible dykes can be explored, and five covered viewing towers and three viewing platforms spread throughout the area provide great lookouts. The dykes define four large, separated marshes, all ripe with life.

One of the best trails for bird activities is along the Nature Dyke Trail, where salmonberry, blackberry and other shrubs encroach onto the path, attracting many songbirds into the dense brush. More than 90 songbird species have been recorded in the area, including orange-crowned, Townsend's, black-throated grey and yellow warblers. Wood ducks and hooded mergansers use the nest boxes installed along this dyke. In the winter many more waterfowl descend onto the wetlands of the management area, as do mute, tundra and trumpeter swans.

Although generally rare in the Lower Mainland, the grey catbird is commonly seen throughout the Pitt-Addington Marsh Wildlife Management Area, which is one of the only known breeding locations of this species along coastal British Columbia. The area also supports the largest concentration of osprey in the Lower Mainland. You can find them nesting on the pilings that line the Pitt River.

Dragonflies zip across the dykes catching insects on the wing. Look out for the western pondhawk, dot-tailed whiteface and blue dasher along the far dyke of the Katzie Marsh. About 250 species of plant have been identified in the Pitt-Addington Marsh, including Labrador tea, bog-laurel, hardhack, bur-reed and bladderwort.

Within the park is the specially designated Pitt Polder Ecological Reserve, which protects 88 hectares of the rapidly disappearing Fraser Valley boglands. This designation is crucial, because it allows the highest level of protection for important habitat in the province.

↑ Grey catbirds are locally rare along coastal British Columbia but are found nesting in this hot spot.

↖ Many kilometres of raised dykes through wetland habitat make for a birding paradise.

Shannon Falls Provincial Park

Melted glacial water carved through granite has created a majestic waterfall

What Makes This Hot Spot Hot?

- The cascading Shannon Falls is the third-highest waterfall in British Columbia.
- A hike or gondola ride takes visitors to the mountain vista, from which the source of the falls can be seen.
- Hiking in the park's subalpine environment can be a magical chance for wildlife viewing.

Address: Sea-to-Sky Hwy (Hwy 99), 3 km south of Squamish, BC
Tel.: (1-800) 689-9025
Websites: www.env.gov. bc.ca/bcparks/explore/ parkpgs/shannon, www.seatoskygondola.com

GPS Coordinates
Latitude: 49.66997
Longitude: −123.15644

Open year-round

♿ (Check ahead)

→ **The falls are visible from the highway, but the quick hike in to get a closer look is well worth it.**

Just south of Stawamus Chief Provincial Park, Shannon Falls plummets a spectacular 335 metres, making it the third-highest waterfall in British Columbia. This breathtaking waterfall is accessed by a leisurely 5-minute walk from the parking lot. This short stroll through coastal forest leads to the base of the falls where cascading water churns in the rocky riverbed and eventually flows into the ocean. The waterfall is fed by melting snow and glaciers from the surrounding mountains and, as such, is at its most powerful on warm spring days. Many visitors choose to walk to the base and then spend a relaxed afternoon in the picnic area.

Shannon Falls is an important place to the Squamish First Nation. There are tales of a two-headed serpent named *Say-noth-ka* carving a path through the granite and creating the falls by repeatedly travelling up and down the mountain. The name of the park and falls come from William Shannon, who sourced clay from the land

to make bricks. The area was later used for logging, which is evidenced by the notches you can see in the large stumps on which loggers placed platforms to stand on while felling towering cedar and fir trees. Following the period of logging, the land was donated to BC Parks in 1982.

For a bird's-eye view, hike or take the Sea to Sky Gondola to the alpine environment above the falls. From this vantage point, the picturesque mountains that feed the falls become visible. There are a number of hiking trails and a suspension bridge with viewpoints of Howe Sound and Squamish. The Wonderland Lake Loop, in particular, is a spectacular hike. On the trail you will see blueberry bushes and alpine flowers and visit a small alpine lake. Keep an eye and an ear out for the sooty grouse, a well-camouflaged ground bird. These birds have unique-sounding calls — the male with his low-pitched hoot and the female with her cackle.

← Sooty grouse are often heard on the trails.

↑ After a quick gondola ride or steep hike, the suspension bridge offers visitors panoramic views of the surrounding mountains, including Sky Pilot and Copilot, both of which feed Shannon Falls with their snow melt.

Skwelwil'em Squamish Estuary

A combined effort by the Squamish Nation and the Ministry of the Environment keeps this area a wild sanctuary

What Makes This Hot Spot Hot?

- Glacial water from the Squamish River meets the ocean in Howe Sound in this estuarine environment.
- The diverse marine and forest habitats in this small area support a variety of life.
- Many species of fish, including the historically important eulachon, use the estuary and Squamish River for spawning.

Address: Spit Road, Squamish, BC
Tel.: (604) 815-4994
Website: www.squamish.ca/our-services/environment-and-sustainability/estuary

GPS Coordinates
Latitude: 49.70472
Longitude: −123.17351

Open year-round

Some rivers carry life-sustaining nutrients from watersheds to the ocean. An estuary, where river meets ocean, becomes a sanctuary of brackish water that supports an abundance of life, creating a splendid opportunity for exploration that will delight any naturalist. The Skwelwil'em Squamish Estuary is no exception. The area sustains diverse habitats — the grassy marshes, open mudflats and hemlock forests support over 200 species of birds alone. Kingfishers, shorebirds like spotted sandpipers and songbirds like the marsh wren and common yellowthroat can all be seen within a short walk. Mammals, including the water shrew, black-tailed deer, coyote and black bear, also frequent the estuary. Keen's myotis, a red-listed species that is one of 16 bat species in British Columbia, roosts in the nearby hemlock forests.

Referred to as the nurseries

↑ The song sparrow is one of the many voices you will hear along the trails.

↓ Black bears frequent the estuary and surrounding forest.

of the sea, estuaries play an important role in fish spawning. Many marine animals spend at least a portion of their life cycle in these nurseries. The waters of the Squamish Estuary host four species of spawning Pacific salmon: chinook, coho, chum and pink. Beneath the surface also swims a small, silver fish called a eulachon, which is about the length of a human hand. Eulachon spawn in the Squamish River and, historically, played an important role in the diets of the Coastal First Nations. This fatty fish was often fried or smoked and eaten immediately. In some cases its fat was extracted and stored for cold winters since the fat does not spoil and is very high in vitamin content. The population of eulachon has declined significantly as ocean temperatures have risen and human encroachment has affected major breeding grounds.

The estuary acts as a sponge for both nutrients and pollutants, which makes it a sensitive environment. By protecting our watersheds we can ensure that this estuary, as well as other estuaries, remains safe for the many species that call this unique ecosystem home.

↑ **Estuary visitors will find stunning views of the surrounding mountains at any time of the year.**

Stanley Park

One of the world's most famous urban parks, Stanley Park has much nature to explore just a stone's throw from downtown Vancouver

What Makes This Hot Spot Hot?

- The park has been deemed an Important Bird Area for the conservation of birds and biodiversity.
- It hosts one of the largest great blue heron nesting colonies in all of North America.
- The Stanley Park Ecological Society offers programs for all ages to enhance your nature experience.

Address: 2099 Beach Avenue, Vancouver, BC
Tel.: (604) 873-7000
Website: www.vancouver. ca/parks-recreation-culture/ stanley-park.aspx

GPS Coordinates
Latitude: 49.29232
Longitude: –123.14586

Open year-round

♿ (Check ahead)

➜ **Looking like an illustration from a children's book, the herons' beach ball-sized nests fill the trees near the Vancouver Board of Parks and Recreation offices.**

Stanley Park is recognized as one of the world's best urban parks — its 400 hectares of diverse land is a natural oasis close to downtown Vancouver. Half a million trees, beautiful beaches and easily accessed intertidal life make this an urban park worth exploring with binoculars and pocket ID books.

The famous seawall is the world's longest uninterrupted waterfront path, allowing for perfect views of Burrard Inlet and English Bay. Stanley Park was established as a city park in 1888, and some things have never changed: biking in the park has been popular since the early 1900s.

The Stanley Park Ecological Society provides many wonderful nature programs that add even more opportunity for nature-based family fun.

As an internationally recognized Important Bird Area, Stanley Park is a birder's paradise. A part of the Pacific Flyway, spring migration brings waves of diverse avian life. In the fall and winter large rafts of overwintering Barrow's goldeneye come to the protected waters in and around Stanley Park. British Columbia is home to 60 per cent of the world's population of this duck species, and their large wintering colonies are worth a wet winter stroll through the park.

Another must-see birding spectacle takes place just outside the Vancouver Board of Parks and Recreation offices. Stanley Park's coastal great blue heron colony is one of the largest nesting colonies of this species in all of North America. This colony is of special importance because, although great blue herons are widespread across the globe, this particular

subspecies is non-migratory and depends on local sites for safe nesting and feeding. As a result of disturbance and habitat loss, the coastal great blue heron is blue-listed and likely close to endangered.

Great blue heron colonies have been recorded in the park since 1921, and today the colony is composed of 80 to 100 pairs. Although the heron nests are high up in the canopy, you can still get a glimpse into the private lives of these prehistoric-looking nestlings by tuning into the park's heron cam on the city's website.

The chicks are fed for about 60 days at the nest with hatching spread out over the early spring, so there are ample opportunities throughout the spring to witness this urban birding extravaganza. Once the chicks have grown a little more they may be seen feeding with adults outside the nest as early as June, with all young leaving the nest before August's end.

↑ An adult great blue heron flies down to the water in search of a meal to bring home to its hungry chicks.

↖ An aerial view of Stanley Park reveals its truly impressive size.

Stawamus Chief Provincial Park

BC Parks and the province's rock climbers merge the sport of rock climbing with environmental preservation

What Makes This Hot Spot Hot?

- The Stawamus Chief stands over the town of Squamish and can be seen from nearly everywhere in the valley.
- Peregrine falcons nest on rocky ledges and outcrops in March and April.
- The top of the Stawamus Chief affords magnificent views of the surrounding mountains and the ocean.

Address: Sea-to-Sky Hwy (Hwy 99), Squamish, BC
Tel.: (604) 986-9371
Website: www.env.gov.bc.ca/bcparks/explore/parkpgs/stawamus

GPS Coordinates
Latitude: 49.67865
Longitude: −123.15457

Open year-round

↗ **The view from the top of the hiking trail, looking over the beautiful turquoise waters of Howe Sound.**

Towering over the Squamish Valley, the Stawamus Chief is an abruptly vertical 700-metre high granite dome. The face of this volcanic rock was slowly carved and polished by glaciers, which has made the park's impressive namesake a popular destination for rock climbers from around the world.

The hiking trails to its three peaks are clearly marked from the main parking lot. Fairly steep but well maintained with stairs, the first peak is generally hiked as a round trip in two to three hours. The trail will guide you through fir and cedar forests alongside a small creek. There are no open areas along the way, which makes the vista all the more breathtaking upon reaching the top. From the first peak, hikers are rewarded for their hard work with a magnificent view of Howe Sound and the nearby mountains. While many visitors conquer just

the first peak, trails at the top lead to the other two peaks. In the summer months the ocean reflects a turquoise blue as a result of the silty glacial water flowing in from the Squamish River. At the mouth of the river, which enters the ocean from the north, you will see a large, open area. This is the Skwelwil'em Squamish Estuary — worth a visit once you return to sea level for its spectacular birding opportunities and scenery, which includes a stunning view of the Chief itself.

Peregrine falcons have chosen the Stawamus Chief as a nesting site, and measures are taken to protect the endangered bird during this sensitive time. Certain climbing routes are closed during nesting season in March and April. This is a good time to bring your binoculars to the open grassy area near the main parking lot and look for falcons on the rock face. Also keep your eyes skywards: the peregrine falcon is the fastest animal in the world, flying at speeds of up to 300 kilometres per hour, and it mainly preys on other birds.

⬆ **The peregrine falcon, which is found nesting here in March and April, is the fastest animal in the world.**

↖ **Stawamus Chief towers over the town of Squamish.**

Whistler Olympic Park

For the nature and sports enthusiasts Whistler Olympic Park offers sights and sounds on well-maintained ski and snowshoe trails

What Makes This Hot Spot Hot?

- Visitors can snowshoe or ski through alpine forests and meadows while enjoying breathtaking views of the coastal mountains.
- In the summer hikers enjoy a different experience as they stroll through the same meadows and past streams and wetlands.
- The oldest cedar trees in the Sea-to-Sky Corridor line some of the trails.

Address: 5 Callaghan Road, Whistler, BC
Tel.: (604) 964-0060
Website:
www.whistlersportlegacies.com/venues/whistler-olympic-park

GPS Coordinates
Latitude: 50.13948
Longitude: –123.11361

Open seasonally, weather permitting. Check the website for hours and conditions

🚶 🔭 🚴 ⛷ 🎽

♿ **(Check ahead)**

→ **The variety of cross-country ski trails will delight both beginner and expert skiers.**

Whistler Olympic Park, in the Madeley Creek basin, was home to the Nordic events at the 2010 Olympic Winter Games. The park is a spectacular place to try snowshoeing or cross-country skiing, as trails are well maintained and the area is patrolled. This does mean, however, a fee is required to enjoy the park.

Against the backdrop of surrounding mountains, the cross-country ski and snowshoe trails wind through forests, marshes and meadows. In the winter there are seemingly endless paths to explore. The snowshoe trails cover both old- and second-growth forests, and the oldest cedar trees in the Sea-to-Sky Corridor line the route along the Real Life Snowshoe Trail. Expect to see the branches of hemlock and fir trees collecting snow, which muffles noise and creates the feeling of a winter wonderland.

There is no shortage of beautiful views on the park's trails. Stop in one of the many viewpoints to behold stunning vistas of the surrounding mountains, such as the distinctive Black Tusk, which sits in nearby Garibaldi Provincial Park. One of the

most spectacular snowshoe routes in the park is the Alexander Falls Trail, which takes hikers to the base of a 17-metre waterfall. Depending on the time of year, the falls may be a tower of frozen ice.

Whistler Olympic Park can also be enjoyed during the summer months on the hiking and biking trails through the forests, meadows and wetlands. The park is surrounded by rugged wilderness and is a small part of a larger ecosystem that supports many birds and mammals, such as weasels, bobcats and moose. During the summer months bears are occasionally sighted, and American dippers and other birds frequent the streams and wetlands of the area.

For those experienced in backcountry travel, the park is an access point to the surrounding mountains and offers day-trip opportunities via ski or snowshoe.

↑ Lakes and mountain views throughout the park reward hikers and cross-country skiers.

→ Alexander Falls is beautiful in both summer and winter.

U.S.A. Stewart

37

7

Cedarvale

Nisga'a Hwy

16

3 Smithers

16

Dixon Entrance

Graham I.

5

Gwaii Haanas
National Park
Reserve and Haida
Heritage Site

Hecate Strait

Bella
Coola

2

*Queen
Charlotte
Sound*

PACIFIC
OCEAN

Vancouver Island

N
W   E
S

Central British Columbia

Dawson Creek

ALBERTA

Tumbler Ridge

Prince George

Upper Fraser

McBride

Bowron Lake Provincial Park

Cariboo Mountains Provincial Park

Mount Robson

Mount Robson Provincial Park

Wells Gray Provincial Park

Williams Lake

Clearwater

Clinton

Ancient Forest/Chun T'oh Whudujut Provincial Park

A northern stand of inland old-growth temperate rainforest that is home to 1,000-year-old trees

What Makes This Hot Spot Hot?

- Part of the Interior Wet Belt, this is the farthest known inland temperate rainforest in the world.
- Some of the massive western redcedars are thought to be 2,000 years old.
- Around 900 plant species have been identified in the park, including a rare bog orchid.

Address: Yellowhead Hwy (Hwy 16) East, 115 km east of Prince George and 103 km west of McBride, BC
Tel.: N/A
Website: www.env.gov.bc.ca/bcparks/explore/parkpgs/ancient-forest

GPS Coordinates
Latitude: 53.763227
Longitude: −121.218708

Open year-round

♿ (Check ahead)

Situated along the northern limits of the Interior Wet Belt, this stand of trees protected within the boundary of Chun T'oh Whudujut (also known as Ancient Forest) Provincial Park is part of the farthest inland old-growth temperate rainforest known to date, located some 800 kilometres from the ocean. One reason these massive redcedars can thrive so far from the coast is thanks to the heavy snowfall that descends on the forest in the winter. The deep snowpack melts in the spring, restoring water supplies in the groundwater, springs and flooding areas of the forest floor.

Aging the trees becomes quite difficult after they have achieved their great size. Although the trees remain alive, giant redcedars often become hollow with age. The heartwood of a tree provides structural support but is composed of dead cells, so living tissue can still thrive around a hollow core, remaining the vital conduit between roots and canopy. Some of the trees in the area are upwards of 1,000 years old, and some timeworn giants may be closer to 2,000 years old, their age an unsolvable mystery. This truly is an ancient forest.

Trees of this great maturity attract a special array of flora and fauna. The park is home to over 200 species of lichen alone! A notable favourite is the gold dust lichen, which encrusts the weathered and paled cedar trunks and gilds the forest with an extra layer of life. Devil's club inhabits much of the undergrowth. The stems and leaves of this plant are covered with a dense armour of needle-like spines that are extremely irritating if touched. This gives visitors one more reason to stay on the trails, though protecting this rare ecosystem is surely reason enough. During a biological assessment of the park's

plant life, bog adder's-mouth orchids were discovered in the area — the first time this rare species had been documented in the Interior since 1932. The red-listed Joe-pye weed is also found within the boundaries of the park.

This magnificent forest was very close to certain destruction but exists today thanks to many passionate individuals working together to ensure the giant trees remained. In 2005 Dave Radies, a graduate student studying old-growth forests of the Interior Cedar-Hemlock Zone, stumbled across this stand and saw telltale forester's red spray-painted on numerous trunks,

which meant some of these ancient trees were tagged for removal. After he alerted the public of this special area and its solemn fate, the community rallied together. The following year the Ancient Forest Trail was built by devoted volunteers, and two years after that the harvesting plans were cancelled. The area was officially designated a provincial park in 2016. The 450-metre boardwalk of the Universal Access Trail ensures that everyone gets to enjoy this unique forest nestled between mountain ranges along the Rocky Mountain Trench.

↑ Devil's club creates dense, and uninviting, undergrowth.

↓ Gold dust lichen covers the trunk of many of the old-growth cedars of this forest.

GREAT BEAR RAINFOREST

Bella Coola Valley

The Great Bear Rainforest is famous for the elusive Kermode bear

What Makes This Hot Spot Hot?

- The Great Bear Rainforest is one of the world's largest remaining coastal temperate rainforests.
- The rainforest is home to the greatest density of grizzly bears in Canada, as well as the rare Kermode bear, a white black bear.
- During spawning season some salmon runs overlap, so multiple species of salmon are often seen travelling upstream at the same time.

Address: Chilcotin-Bella Coola Hwy (Hwy 20), Bella Coola Valley, BC
Tel.: (250) 799-5202
Website: www.bellacoola.ca

GPS Coordinates
Latitude: 52.379280
Longitude: −126.763960

Open year-round

The Bella Coola Valley acts as a gateway into the Great Bear Rainforest and is the perfect destination for a memorable bear-watching adventure. With the valley stretching 80 kilometres along the Bella Coola River, the small community here and the surrounding area can be reached by land, air and sea, including ferry services.

Grizzly bears and black bears are found throughout the Bella Coola Valley and adjoining Tweedsmuir Park. The Great Bear Rainforest, one of the world's largest intact coastal temperate rainforests, is home to a special population of black bears. One in every 10 black bears here has a cream-coloured coat, thanks to a recessive gene found in this particular population. These dramatic white bears are not albino, and both parents have to carry and pass on the gene for the offspring to be white. Catching a glimpse of a Kermode bear is one of British Columbia's most sought-after and unique nature-viewing experiences, and although uncommon,

there is always a chance one will reveal itself along the river's edge as it hunts for fish.

The Great Bear Rainforest supports Canada's largest and densest population of grizzly bears, who depend on the large intact forest since much of their historic range has dramatically shrunk. The grizzlies of the coast are much larger than their Interior relatives, thanks to the easy access of spawning salmon each fall. The largest males have been recorded to weigh over 500 kilograms after their fishy autumn feast! Aside from being generally much larger, grizzlies can be distinguished from brown-phase black bears by their pronounced shoulder humps, formed by strong digging muscles, as well as their prominent claws and wider, rounder faces.

Visitors can expect to see bears in the valley throughout the spring and well into fall. In the spring, watch for bears feeding on new plant roots and shoots, or plan your trip around the salmon spawn between late July and early October to see grizzlies and black bears feasting on salmon

in the rivers and streams. Mid-August to late September will likely provide the best viewing opportunities. To avoid conflict with the larger, more aggressive grizzlies, black bears tend to drag their fish farther into the forest, which in turn provides important nutrients to this habitat.

Visitors often spot bears while driving and occasionally while hiking throughout the Bella Coola Valley, but the best way to guarantee safe and successful viewing is to book a bear-watching tour. Some tours are by boats and rafts that drift along through the salmon spawns to areas where bears are known to feed, while others take you on hikes to view bears from land. Going with a guide is highly recommended, and there are plenty of options to plan a trip that suits your needs.

↑ The Kermode bear is a rare and thrilling sight in the Bella Coola Valley.

↓ Sibling grizzlies find time to play and wrestle while feasting on the spawning salmon.

HUDSON BAY MOUNTAIN

Crater Lake Trail

A short hike takes you up into the alpine and right into mountain goat territory

What Makes This Hot Spot Hot?

- There is a great chance of seeing mountain goats in the area.
- Horned larks nest in the alpine meadows.
- A beautiful tarn lake greets you at the top of the hike.

Address: 3866 Railway Avenue, Smithers, BC
Tel.: (250) 847-2058
Website: www.tourismsmithers.com/directory/hudson-bay-mountain-trails

GPS Coordinates
Latitude: 54.769671
Longitude: −127.279285

Open year-round

 (Check ahead)

↗ **A mountain goat and her kid lounge on a rocky slope.**

Although Hudson Bay Mountain attracts most of its visitors in the form of sports enthusiasts exploring its snow-covered mountainside, this area is also a summer destination for nature lovers. As the drive to the ski hill already brings you to a high elevation, it is not too long before you are nestled in delightful alpine meadows after a short, but mosquito-dense, hike through the last stretch of the treeline. A small reflective tarn called Crater Lake is your destination: a charming little lake nestled in the amphitheatre-like cirque that was carved by a glacier long since melted. Watch for hoary marmots, which will surely be watching as you cross through exposed meadows.

Plan your trip with the bloom times for alpine wildflowers in mind, and you will be rewarded with blankets of blue, pink, yellow and white flowers. Pink and white mountain-heathers carpet the area, each colour seemingly claiming separate parcels of land as its own. Look out for green false hellebore, forget-me-nots and Alaska violets along the trail. Sedums, like the western

roseroot, can be found flowering well above the treeline, where moss campion also clings to the barren landscape.

Of course, these plants are displaying showy flowers for a reason, and the harsh, exposed environment does not deter robust bumble bees. The large size and fuzzy bodies of bumbles help them retain heat as they travel from flower to flower collecting pollen in their baskets. Their meticulous work helps to ensure that wildflowers will bloom in the meadows for years to come.

Horned larks are a highlight of this alpine adventure as their musical song can be heard ringing out across the meadow. In the summer keep an eye out for fledgling larks nestled low to the ground while they wait for an adult to return with food. Horned larks begin nesting as soon as snow-free patches appear in the meadows, constructing fine woven baskets to house their families. Sometimes females will create "pavings" beside their nests, a small collection of pebbles, clods of soil and other materials that resembles a walkway.

This region is home to a healthy population of mountain goats that frequents the slopes of Hudson Bay Mountain between June and October, although the best time to spot them is August and September. Among the world's most skilled mountaineers, these agile ungulates usually stay close to cliffs so that they can make a quick escape up often near-vertical slopes to safety.

↑ A fledgling horned lark blends into the alpine groundcover.

↖ Crater Lake, your rewarding destination after a hike.

TUMBLER RIDGE GLOBAL GEOPARK

Flatbed Cabin Pools Trail

Dinosaur trackways are visible right along the trail by Flatbed Creek

What Makes This Hot Spot Hot?

- Visitors can follow theropod, ornithopod and ankylosaur trackways on this 3-kilometre return hike.
- A nearby bone bed is Western Canada's oldest-known dinosaur material.
- Many other special fossils have been found in the geopark, from Precambrian to Cretaceous.

Address: 1 km southeast of Tumbler Ridge, Don Phillips Way (Hwy 29), Tumbler Ridge, BC
Tel.: (250) 242-3123
Website: www.tumblerridgegeopark.ca/index.php/fossil-sites

GPS Coordinates
Latitude: 55.114361
Longitude: −120.983255

Open year-round

Ankylosaurs walked on all fours and their hind footprints almost covered their front, leaving crescent-shaped prints. Look for five toes on the leading edge of a larger four-toed hind print.

Along the eastern slopes of the Rocky Mountains, you will find Tumbler Ridge Global Geopark, the first park with this designation in western North America. Although the geopark title holds no protection for the land within its boundaries, Gwillim Lake, Bearhole Lake, Wapiti Lake and Monkman provincial parks all fall at least partially within the geopark.

The geological formations here range from the Precambrian to Cretaceous periods and include much more recent Pleistocene deposits. Many fossils can be found within the park boundaries, from Cretaceous dinosaur trackways and bone beds to Triassic fishes and marine reptiles. Dinosaur bones in the area span nearly 60 million years. The local Dinosaur Discovery Gallery has many fossils, imprints and casts on display, but visitors are able to check out some of the fossil sites to get a first-hand experience of these prehistoric remains.

In 2000, two local boys discovered a dinosaur trackway while water tubing along Flatbed Creek. This led to an explosion of additional finds in the surrounding area. In fact,

→ A view of Flatbed Creek, where two boys water tubing down the creek led to the discovery of dinosaur trackways near the water.

many fossils were discovered by amateur fossil enthusiasts! Fossils are still being found, so if you think you may have discovered a new dinosaur footprint or bone, leave it be and contact Peace River Region Palaeontology Research Centre at (250) 242-DINO or email prprc@pris.ca.

Tracks of three kinds of dinosaurs have been found in Tumbler Ridge: ankylosaurs, known for sometimes having large clubbed tails; theropods, bipedal dinosaurs built for speed; and ornithopods, grazers that used their stiff tails for balance. Be careful not to walk directly on any of the footprints so that you do not speed up their erosion.

The original 26 ankylosaur prints of Flatbed Creek are only accessible when the creek water level is low, and they are now very faint as they continue to be weathered by natural water flows. In addition to the Flatbed Cabin Pools Trail, dinosaur tracks can be seen on the Wolverine Dinosaur Trail, although unguided exploration is discouraged. Tours can be booked for both sites through the Tumbler Ridge Museum Foundation by calling the Dinosaur Discovery Gallery. A special evening lantern-lit tour is offered for the Wolverine Trail, where tracks barely visible by day are revealed in low light.

Although fossils are the main attraction of the Flatbed Cabin Pools Trail, scan the surrounding understory for wildflowers blooming in the early summer, and peek through the trees near the start of the trail to catch a glimpse of a massive bog. Watch for black bears throughout the geopark as they feed on vegetation along the roadside.

↓ Theropods left narrow, three-toed prints, occasionally with claw marks visible at the ends of their long toes. In this fossilized track, you can see the dewclaw print it left behind.

GWAII HAANAS NATIONAL PARK RESERVE, NATIONAL MARINE CONSERVATION AREA RESERVE AND HAIDA HERITAGE SITE

Gwaii Haanas

Protected from sea floor to mountaintop, with rainforests blanketed in moss, intertidal zones teeming with wildlife and many of its own subspecies, this park reserve is a treasure for all

What Makes This Hot Spot Hot?

- The lush, ancient rainforest filled with towering cedars inspired Haida activists to lobby to get the southern third of the Haida Gwaii archipelago protected.
- Many distinct and endemic subspecies call these isolated islands home.
- Heritage sites are found throughout the protected area containing art and architecture that highlights the rich history of the Haida Nation.

Address: Haida Gwaii, BC
Tel.: (1-877) 559-8818
Website: www.pc.gc.ca/en/pn-np/bc/gwaiihaanas

GPS Coordinates
Latitude: 52.46827
Longitude: −131.5596

Open year-round

↗ **Humpback whales feed in the chilly waters of the Pacific Northwest.**

Haida Gwaii is a large archipelago separated from British Columbia's west coast. Hecate Strait, which runs up to 140 kilometres across, isolates Haida Gwaii from the Mainland, creating a barrier that has segregated wildlife to the islands. Evolving in isolation, 39 subspecies of plants and animals found nowhere else in the world thrive here. This includes the Haida Gwaii black bear, which has superior jaw strength to its Mainland counterpart — better for crushing hard-shelled critters in the intertidal zone.

Birders, botanizers and marine enthusiasts will all find something to delight them on these islands. Although the number of bird species, approximately 300, is lower than the adjacent Mainland's, there are more unique types to spot, such as the yellow-billed loon and the short-tailed albatross. During the last ice age British Columbia was blanketed in glaciers; however, back then, parts of Haida Gwaii remained uncovered or were only coated in a thin layer of ice and snow. As a result, some plants here were unaffected by glaciation and quickly repopulated the islands, making this environment particularly special.

Gwaii Haanas National Park Reserve, National Marine Conservation Area Reserve and Haida Heritage Site is the perfect place to experience the wonders of this archipelago. This vast park reserve offers kayaking opportunities to explore the area by water as well as hiking trails, campsites and cultural heritage sites, including those of the Haida Nation that date back some 14,000 years. Visit Hlk'yah GaawGa, where in 2013 a monumental pole was erected to acknowledge the 20th anniversary of

the Gwaii Haanas Agreement and the continued cooperative work between the Council of the Haida Nation and Parks Canada. After resident Haida blocked roads to protest the logging of the archipelago's ancient rainforests, the Gwaii Haanas Agreement was established by the Government of Canada and the Council of the Haida Nation to cooperatively manage and protect the cultural and natural treasures of this area.

Haida Gwaii can be accessed only by boat or seaplane. Your visit to Gwaii Haanas will not be interrupted by the sounds of cars since there are no roads in the park reserve. To enter, you must reserve a spot, attend a mandatory orientation about travel, safety and the natural and cultural history of the region, and then receive a trip permit.

↑ Lush rainforests of towering cedar surround boardwalks and trails.

⬉ Poles found on SGang Gwaay mark what was once a community of 300 Haida people.

Mount Robson Provincial Park

This park is named for a breathtaking peak that towers over meadows, forests and clear alpine streams

What Makes This Hot Spot Hot?

- The park protects the headwaters of the Fraser River, which brings life to much of British Columbia.
- Drastic changes in elevation encourage diverse ecosystems, flora and fauna.
- Mount Robson is the tallest of the Canadian Rocky Mountains and has a rich history among the First Nations in the area as well as mountain climbers.

Address: Off Yellowhead Hwy (Hwy 16), 33 km northeast of Valemont, Fraser-Fort George, BC
Tel.: (250) 566-4038
Website: www.env.gov.bc.ca/bcparks/explore/parkpgs/mt_robson

GPS Coordinates
Latitude: 53.03385
Longitude: −119.23158

Open year-round

♿ (Check ahead)

This UNESCO World Heritage Site is home to the highest mountain in the Canadian Rockies, which is also the second-highest in British Columbia. At 2,975 metres, Mount Robson, the park's namesake, is a spectacular rock face. Because of the horizontal strips of coloured rock — limestone, dolomite and quartzite — the people of the Texqakallt Nation refer to the peak as *Yuh-hai-has-kun*, or "the Mountain of the Spiral Road."

Established in 1913 and charged with the important task of protecting the headwaters of the mighty Fraser River, this park is the second-oldest in British Columbia. Downstream, the Fraser River flows through many other nature hot spots before entering the ocean in Vancouver. The river provides life to a large portion of the province in the form of

nutrients, spawning ground, food and water. It is amazing to think that it all begins in this park. Hikers can explore the river's origins on the gentle Fraser River Nature Walk.

There is a wide variety of ecosystems within the park and an abundance of splendid views and wildlife to discover. Each June the park hosts its annual Bird Blitz when birders come together to count the species of birds in the park. There is no shortage, with over 180 recorded species found — including golden eagles in the alpine tundra environment. Elk, bears, Rocky Mountain bighorn sheep and moose live here, among other animals. Bring binoculars if you have them, not just for the birds but also to watch for mountain goats on the surrounding cliffs. The plant life here is not inconspicuous either. Lupine, thimbleberry, redcedar, lodgepole pine and spruce are all found at varying elevations.

Mount Robson Provincial Park deserves a few days, and the Robson Meadows Campground is a fantastic place to make base camp. From there you can explore the wetlands, meadows, forests and alpine environments on the park's many trails.

↑ Lucky hikers may catch a glimpse of a Rocky Mountain bighorn sheep.

↖ Mount Robson towers over the surrounding forest.

← Fields of lupine and other wildflowers paint the alpine meadows.

Nisga'a Memorial Lava Bed Provincial Park

The dramatic landscape resulting from one of Canada's most recent volcanic eruptions is rich in both history and species diversity

What Makes This Hot Spot Hot?

- Explore a landscape that, less than 300 years ago, was the site of a devastating volcanic eruption that buried villages and changed the area forever.
- Unique log moulds were created when molten rock cooled around the trunks of trees that were surrounded and toppled by the lava flow.
- This truly unique park elegantly weaves the natural and cultural histories of the Nisga'a Nation's amazing land.

Address: Aiyansh, Nisga'a Hwy (Hwy 113), BC
Tel.: (250) 638-8490
Website: www.env.gov. bc.ca/bcparks/explore/ parkpgs/nisgaa

GPS Coordinates
Latitude: 55.095140
Longitude: −128.970552

Open year-round

🧍 🦌 ⛺

♿ (Check ahead)

Almost 300 years ago, a volcanic eruption burst forth from the Tseax Cone. As molten rock spilled from the crater, it covered everything in its path, including two Nisga'a villages, and tragically killed more than 2,000 people. Nisga'a Memorial Lava Bed Provincial Park (also known as Anhluut'ukwsim Laxmihl Angwinga'asanskwhl Nisga'a), which is co-managed by the Nisga'a people and BC Parks, remains a memorial site for those lost, an amazing opportunity to learn about the Nisga'a Nation and their history, and a chance to experience a unique nature hot spot.

The expansive lava beds still dominate the landscape, providing an opportunity to investigate the slow and dramatic return of life to this harsh, barren landscape. Lichens were the first species to establish on the lava rock, encrusting the rough rubble. Over time the lichen growth thickened, and trapped leaves, dirt and debris built up in the crevices, allowing other species to move in. Although vast portions of the lava fields still only support lichens and a few tough, low-lying plants, areas near water sustain the growth of large trees and a healthy forest community. In some areas, the lava rock is 12 metres deep and buries the rushing waters of Lax Mihl (Crater Creek), which still flows through underground passageways.

Beautiful falls found within the park are easily

◂ **Ksiluuyim Agiiy (Vetter Falls) cascades artfully into turquoise waters.**

↪ **Visitors will find unique log moulds, which were created when lava quickly cooled around engulfed trees.**

accessed through short, flat, well-maintained trails. Do not miss the opportunity to take in the breathtaking sight of white, rushing water hitting the calmer flow of a turquoise stream, surrounded by dense conifers and a moss-covered forest floor. Ksiluuyim Agiiy (Vetter Falls) is a stunning set of waterfalls where glacier-fed waters spill over a short ledge before continuing downstream.

Among the most fascinating lava formations found in the park are log moulds. As the lava flowed across the landscape and destroyed everything in its path, it surrounded, toppled and burned large trees. In some cases, when the lava cooled quickly enough around a tree, it formed a mould of the tree. The trees burned or eventually rotted away, leaving dramatic hollow tubes on the landscape. This area is also a great place to examine some small but tough inhabitants of the lava beds. Three-toothed and spotted saxifrage root in the cracks, and the bubbly green and bright red leaves of spreading stonecrop form small mats on even

lava. The Nisga'a call them lava berries for this reason.

The only way to access the Tseax Cone is through a guided hiking tour, allowing for the protection of this important and sensitive area. Tours begin from the visitor centre, which is built in the style of a traditional longhouse with many interpretive displays on the history and culture of the Nisga'a. Make sure you also visit the impressive Nisga'a Museum, Hli Goothl Wilp Adokshl Nisga'a ("the Heart of Nisga'a House Crests"). Here you become immersed in the deep roots and culture of the people, including the long, painful battle for a treaty that acknowledged their claim to this beautiful land they have always called home.

↑ **Vibrant spreading stonecrop creeps across the harsh lava landscape.**

TUMBLER RIDGE GLOBAL GEOPARK

Quality Falls

A beautiful trail to a waterfall is also the site of an important bird discovery

What Makes This Hot Spot Hot?

- Rock formations nearly 100 million years old have resulted in a cascading waterfall.
- This area is an important contact zone between eastern and western bird species.
- Wildflowers can be found all along the trail to the falls.

Address: Heritage Hwy (Hwy 52), Tumbler Ridge, BC
Tel.: (250) 242-3123
Website:
www.tumblerridgegeopark.ca/index.php/project/quality-falls

GPS Coordinates
Latitude: 55.155964
Longitude: −120.939699

Open year-round

↗ **Bunchberries have an explosive pollination strategy. Once triggered, mature, unopened flowers burst open in 0.4 milliseconds and catapult pollen into the air.**

There is much to explore within Tumbler Ridge Global Geopark, as the boundaries incorporate 43 geosites of geological and aesthetic interest. These sites include unique rock formations, canyons, mountain summits, caves and many breathtaking waterfalls. Monkman Provincial Park falls within the boundary of the geopark and has some of the most magnificent waterfalls in northern BC, including the Monkman Cascades — a series of 10 waterfalls within the span of a few kilometres.

However, access to many of these falls are limited to those with extensive backcountry

experience, and some require rugged multiday hikes to reach. Although there are many hiking trails that lead to waterfall views within the geopark boundary, Quality Falls is one of the best options for an easy day-hike that does not require extensive travel down long gravel service roads. The layering of sandstone and shale has created a beautiful formation for the waters of Quality Falls to cascade over, as the shale erodes more easily than the sandstone, creating distinct lips and layers in the rock.

Tumbler Ridge Geopark is impressive not only for its geology but for its ecology as well, as eastern and western bird species overlap on this eastern edge of the Rocky Mountains. Bird enthusiasts may encounter Townsend's, MacGillvray's and Audubon's warblers, as well as their eastern relatives the black-throated green, mourning and myrtle warblers.

Although this contact zone has resulted in a lot of hybridization between closely related species, a special discovery at

Quality Falls actually led to the classification of a distinct species. At the time of this discovery, the winter wrens in British Columbia were considered the same species as those occurring in the rest of Canada. The species was assumed to be geographically separated into eastern and western populations. At the trailhead of this hike, researchers discovered both populations singing their distinct songs within 100 metres of each other. After netting birds of both populations and obtaining blood samples, DNA analysis showed that these two forms did not interbreed and were in fact distinct. As a result, the western population was declared its own species — the Pacific wren.

Tumbler Ridge is also a great place to encounter a mix of western and eastern plant species. In the early summer the trail down to the falls is surrounded with flowering bunchberry, pink wintergreen, tall bluebell and twinflower, the latter a supposed favourite of the 18th century botanist Carl Linnaeus.

↑ The rock formation of Quality Falls is composed of weathered shale and sandstone.

→ The Pacific wren is now its own species after it was encountered singing its distinct song alongside that of its eastern relatives.

Scout Island Nature Centre

In the heart of Williams Lake, a birding paradise awaits

What Makes This Hot Spot Hot?

- The area is frequently visited by American white pelicans.
- A short trail weaves through wetland, shoreline, forest and field.
- A great diversity of nesting birds is found here, from raptors to waterfowl to warblers.

Address: 1305 A Borland Road, Williams Lake, BC
Tel.: (250) 398-8532
Website: www.scoutisland naturecentre.ca

GPS Coordinates
Latitude: 52.120244
Longitude: −122.120437

Open year-round

↗ **During the breeding season, American white pelicans sport a bill horn on their upper bill.**

↗ **A curious common yellowthroat makes its presence known along the trail.**

Visitors to Scout Island Nature Centre in the city of Williams Lake will find a wildlife sanctuary and birder's paradise bursting with avian activity year-round. The centre includes wetland, lake, grassland and woodland habitats.

Operated by the Williams Lake Field Naturalists, this is a wonderful destination for not just nature viewing but also nature education, as the centre offers activities and programs for all ages. Two and a half kilometres of trail will take you through the varied habitats over the 9.69 hectares of protected land. Nest boxes are installed throughout the park to support breeding bird populations, from tree swallows to wood ducks. An osprey pair takes full advantage of the platform installed for them. Bat boxes provide roosting shelter for little brown bats after a busy night catching mosquitoes on the wing.

The early summer provides ample opportunity to watch bird families feeding together. Wood ducks, cinnamon and green-winged teals, and red-necked grebes are just some of the summer residents that breed in the wetland habitat found in the park. Yellow-headed blackbirds are abundant, and the striking plumage of the males makes them easy to spot as they sing while perched on cattails and bulrushes. Bullock's orioles, yellow warblers, common yellowthroats and many other songbirds breed within the wild spaces of Scout Island.

The Cariboo Chilcotin area is home to the only nesting colony of American white pelicans in British Columbia, found within the provincial park protecting Strum Lake, 70 kilometres northwest of Scout Island. Although they do not nest in Williams Lake, they are frequent visitors. There are few fish in Strum Lake, so these giant birds make regular flights to feed at lakes up to 164 kilometres away from their nesting sites. There is a good chance to see these provincially rare birds at Scout Island, and if they are present, they are hard to miss. Their bright white plumage is contrasted with jet-black primary wing feathers. Pelicans are most famous for

their giant, comical orange bill, with an obvious and unusual throat pouch used to hold captured fish before swallowing. Contrary to popular belief, pelicans do not hold food within this pouch for any significant length of time and instead use it to sieve water from food before swallowing. The pouches also help the large birds thermoregulate on hot days. During the breeding season, mature adults grow a strange horn-like projection on their upper bill, reminiscent of the centreboard on the hull of an upturned boat. Look for small groups of pelicans feeding together on the lake or flying overhead. They are surprisingly masterful flyers, despite being one of the heaviest flying birds, and often are seen in V formation, flapping their wings in unison between bouts of graceful gliding.

Wells Gray Provincial Park

Where viewing iconic waterfalls and spotting bears snatching salmon from the river can be combined into a day trip

What Makes This Hot Spot Hot?

- Salmon make an epic journey from Alaska to the BC Interior, where bears feed upon them in the river during spawning.
- A number of scenic waterfalls are found in this landscape, which was sculpted by volcanic action and glaciers.
- As an important wildlife corridor, there are many opportunities to see wildlife while hiking or canoeing.

Address: Clearwater Valley Road, 10 km north of Clearwater, BC
Tel.: (250) 674-3334
Website: www.env.gov.bc.ca/bcparks/explore/parkpgs/wells_gry

GPS Coordinates
Latitude: 51.92815
Longitude: –120.13195

Open year-round

♿ (Check ahead)

Wells Gray Provincial Park protects some of British Columbia's most scenic treasures. Sculpted by glaciers and riddled with volcanic features, this large park in the Interior has expansive stretches of remote wilderness that complement its easily reachable southern section. This combination of accessibility and high-level protection allows the park to thrive, which in turn makes the plants, animals and sights all the more beautiful to behold.

Clearwater Lake, which is surrounded by mountains, is a perfect home base and stunning from both shore and canoe. It was once a large glacier-carved basin that was later dammed by lava and filled with water to create the lake we see today. The outflow of the lake pours over the lava dam, creating Osprey Falls.

Stepping onto one of the park's many trails just off the road, visitors will feel fully immersed in nature, despite being in a popular recreational area. Bears are often sighted alongside creeks hunting for fish. The best time to see them is from August to October, when sockeye

→ **Helmcken Falls is arguably the most majestic waterfall in British Columbia and is easily reachable.**

↙ **Moose and other wildlife roam the park.**

salmon are spawning and the bears emerge from the forest to feed at the river's edge. One of the most impressive places to view this is Bailey's Chute, where the rivers teem with salmon struggling up the fast flowing water.

Well known for its waterfalls, the park hosts the iconic Helmcken Falls, an uninterrupted tower of free-falling water along the Murtle River. Easily one of the most visited sites in the park, this spectacular waterfall is the fourth-highest in Canada and continues to have an amazing impact on the landscape. The rock in the basin where the water falls continues to be carved by the falling water.

For the inquisitive mind there are guided hikes and horseback tours throughout the park, and for the adventurer there are many backcountry trails. The alpine meadows and dense forests are home to many animals. Moose utilize Wells Gray as a winter habitat, roaming through snow-covered forests and across fields. The park also hosts many deer and coyotes.

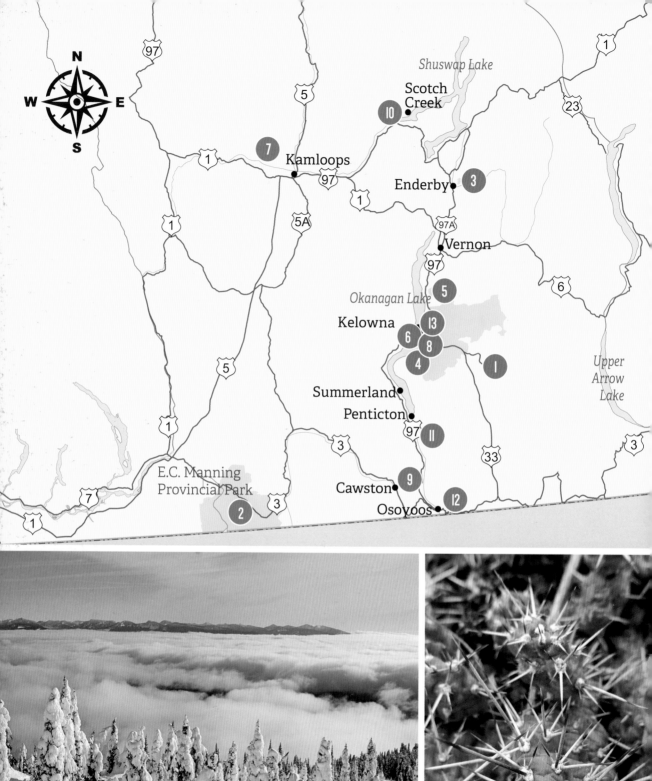

Okanagan, Similkameen and Area

Big White Mountain

Whether summer or winter, the natural beauty of the alpine is always on display in this Okanagan gem

What Makes This Hot Spot Hot?

- The alpine tundra gives visitors spectacular hiking opportunities with stirring views of the surrounding mountains.
- This area is bordered by an ecological reserve, allowing visitors to enjoy this natural space while also providing sanctuary for the plants and wildlife.
- One of British Columbia's treasured winter wonderlands, Big White Ski Resort offers skiing, snowboarding and snowshoeing during the winter.

Address: 5315 Big White Road, Kelowna, BC
Tel.: (250) 765-3101
Website: www.bigwhite.com

GPS Coordinates
Latitude: 49.72161
Longitude: –118.92659

Open for winter activities from late November to early April; open for summer hiking from mid-June to early September; visit the website for specific dates

Big White Mountain is well known as a ski resort by locals in the Okanagan. What many people do not know about are the spectacular winter snowshoeing and summer hiking opportunities for the nature enthusiast. In the summer, alpine flowers, such as mountain arnica and purple lupin, flourish in the grassy meadows, hardy trees surround the trails and the alpine tundra offers delightful views and chances to bird watch. Wildlife thrives here, in large part thanks to Big White Mountain Ecological Reserve just northeast of the resort. The reserve itself does not have any developed trails and serves as an important area for its ecosystems and unique high-elevation wetlands. Stay on the designated hiking trails to help protect this important space.

Hike to the top of the mountain on the Falcon Ridge Trail or to Rhonda Lake on a trail that meanders in and out of the forest. Old-growth stands of spruce trees interspersed with open meadows provide habitat to many unique species of animals, including moose, porcupines, pine martens and bears.

Rhonda Lake is well worth the hike. This beautiful alpine lake makes for a fantastic lunch spot and gives hikers entry to the upper trails, which can be accessed more easily on weekends when the Bullet Chair lift is open. These trails are in the alpine tundra and are too windswept to support the tree growth found at lower elevations. Small, hardy alpine plants dominate and lovely lichens paint the rocks.

Once the area is buried deep in snow, delight in the bluebird days Big White Mountain Ski Resort offers above the layer of wintry clouds that cover the valley. Discover the same spaces in a whole new way. Snowshoeing trails weave through the forest around the mountain's base, and skiers and snowboarders enjoy the alpine.

→ **Meadows of alpine flowers replace blankets of snow in the spring and summer.**

↑ In the winter months Big White is worth a trip just to get above the clouds and into the sunshine.

↓ A pine marten peeks out from behind a tree.

E.C. Manning Provincial Park

Year-round recreational activities encourage visitors to explore the park on foot or by skis and snowshoes

What Makes This Hot Spot Hot?

- Every June a two-day Bird Blitz is hosted in the park, where birders identify the various birds living in the area.
- The park sits on the northernmost section of the famous Pacific Crest Trail.
- People of all hiking abilities can enjoy the mid-summer bloom of alpine flowers as well as river otters playing in nearby bodies of fresh water.

Address: 7500 Crowsnest Hwy (Hwy 3), Manning Park, BC
Tel.: (604) 668-5953
Website: www.env.gov. bc.ca/bcparks/explore/parkpgs/ecmanning

GPS Coordinates
Latitude: 49.08333
Longitude: −120.83333

Open year-round

♿ (Check ahead)

↗ **The view from the Skyline Trail is well worth the effort.**

Lying on the northernmost tip of the Cascade mountain range, E.C. Manning Provincial Park is known as the end of the 4,265-kilometre Pacific Crest Trail that connects Mexico and Canada. The park's location makes it ideal for those travelling between inland British Columbia and the coast to get out and stretch their legs, though it is also a destination for campers and hikers from around the province.

Rhododendron Flats, an easy loop right off the Crowsnest Highway (Highway 3), makes for a spectacular stroll in mid-June. The forest canopy shades areas of beautiful red rhododendrons blooming alongside the trail. Although more challenging, the Skyline Trail affords spectacular views of the surrounding mountains. Lightning Lake, a popular campsite, gives visitors access to many hiking trails as well as the chance to canoe. All of the trails in the park offer abundant wildlife viewing opportunities, with mammals such as deer, moose, bears, hoary marmots and coyotes roaming the park. On the lake and riverside trails, look for sleek river otters in the water or sunning themselves on the banks.

Strawberry Flats is a marvellous place to stop and bird watch. The rufous hummingbird and Canada's tiny calliope hummingbird are often spotted in these open meadows. Other popular birding locations include Beaver Pond, where you may see water-loving birds such as sandpipers. Venture into the alpine area to see the white-tailed ptarmigan or grey-crowned rosy-finch. To access the area follow the Frosty Mountain Trail or hike a section of the Pacific Crest Trail. Alpine flowers are generally in full bloom by mid-summer, so whatever trail you choose to travel along, the flowers provide bursts of colour along your journey. Splashes of brilliant purple from the lupines amid red paintbrushes and an array of pinks and yellows are truly a magical sight.

Winter recreation is a large part of Manning Park. Groomed ski trails allow access to views of snow-covered peaks, and winter campsites immerse travellers in the grandeur of an alpine environment blanketed with snow. Whatever the season prepare to be impressed by the natural beauty of this park.

↑ **Visitors tour Lightning Lake by canoe.**

Enderby Cliffs Provincial Park

Dramatic cliffs of volcanic rock provide a unique habitat for wildlife and a viewing platform for hikers

What Makes This Hot Spot Hot?

- Turkey vultures, red-tailed hawks and eagles soar in updrafts created by the cliff faces.
- Standing atop sheer rock cliffs offers outstanding views of the North Okanagan and Shuswap region.
- The cliffs are tertiary rock formations of lava carved by receding glaciers.

Address: Grindrod, BC
Tel.: (250) 260-3041
Website: www.env.gov. bc.ca/bcparks/explore/ parkpgs/enderby_cliffs

GPS Coordinates
Latitude: 50.57597
Longitude: −119.10456

Open year-round

Escape civilization on the Tplaqin Trail as it weaves its way to the top of Enderby Cliffs. This often-quiet trail is a delight for hikers, naturalists and geology enthusiasts. The picturesque cliffs were formed by glaciers gradually eroding the hardened lava of which the cliffs are composed. The cliffs are topped with tranquil, grassy plateaus that contrast the bare, rocky face. From the top there is a stunning view of the Shuswap and Okanagan valleys.

The rugged but well-marked trail ascends 670 metres through old-growth stands of Douglas-fir, hemlock and larch trees. The forests are occasionally interrupted with grassy fields dotted with ladyslippers and glacier lilies, among other flowers. Nearing the summit the trail leaves the coniferous forest behind, and stands of deciduous trees and small shrubs dominate the open plateaus. Songbirds sing, while golden eagles and red-tailed hawks soar on updrafts. If you have binoculars bring them, but even with the naked eye you cannot miss these magnificent birds. Along with views of birds hikers have a spectacular view of the valley below. The Shuswap River weaves through farmland where the Okanagan and Shuswap valleys meet. From this vantage point the fields appear to be a patchwork quilt of green and yellow squares.

The cliffs are a protected area and host a wide variety of wildlife. The sheer rock faces make them an ideal habitat for bats, swallows and other cliff-dwelling birds. The park extends beyond the trail system, and the vegetation in these isolated sections provides habitat for mule deer, lynx, moose and black and grizzly bears. Keep an eye out in muddy areas along the hike for the tracks of some of these larger mammals. Remember to be respectful of the slow-growing plants in the wind-swept environment by staying on the trail, and be careful of the steep cliff drop-offs.

→ **The vertical cliff faces make a perfect habitat for cliff-dwelling birds and bats.**

Johns Family Nature Conservancy Regional Park

Watch the story of forest succession following a wildfire unfold

What Makes This Hot Spot Hot?

- The Okanagan Mountain Park wildfire burned this park to the ground in 2003, beginning a cycle of forest succession.
- A hike to the top of the rocky bluffs rewards visitors with a panoramic view of Okanagan Lake and the city of Kelowna.
- The rubber boa is frequently seen moving between the rocks beneath the bluffs.

Address: 6970 Chute Lake Road, Kelowna, BC
Tel.: (250) 717-2757
Website: www.regionaldistrict.com/your-services/parks-services/parks-and-trails/30-johns-family-nature-conservancy-regional-park.aspx

GPS Coordinates
Latitude: 49.77392
Longitude: –119.52135

Open year-round

This changing landscape tells the story of forest succession following the Okanagan Mountain Park wildfire. In the 2003 fire Cedar Mountain Regional Park, as it was then known, burned to the ground, including all of the western redcedars for which the park was originally named. In 2013 the Johns family, who owned land near Cedar Mountain, generously donated 323 hectares to the Central Okanagan Land Trust for expanding and preserving the park. To honour this donation the name was changed from Cedar Mountain Regional Park to the Johns Family Nature Conservancy Regional Park.

Although regrowth has been in action for years, the effects of the wildfire remain obvious. Charred standing and fallen trees still cover the park. Immediately following the fire the park was devoid of life and the soil was inhospitable for plant growth. Nitrogen-fixing plants such as fireweed, clover and alder quickly took root, beginning the succession of the forest. These plants have root-dwelling micro-organisms that move much needed nitrogen into the ground. A decade and a half after the fire, grasses and flowers, along with mushrooms, pine and alder, now shape the landscape. Chocolate lilies have bloomed and the aspen, currently covering much of the treed areas, will eventually give way to cedar, fir and pine, continuing the succession.

As you enter the park follow an established trail and look for a smaller one to the right that leads to the base of the large rock face frequented by Kelowna rock climbers. Here you can choose to hike to the lookout by following the steep trail to the right, or you can explore beneath the rock face.

Alongside plants, animals, too, are reclaiming this area as home. From the littlest crab spider on a tree to a deer munching on leaves, it is not uncommon to see wildlife in this park. You may even

see the rubber boa, a true constrictor, in among the rocks. Rubber boas are a harmless, greenish-brown snake and do not bite. When threatened they will curl into a ball, hiding their heads and poking out their tail as a decoy, quick to surrender under any real threat. Due to human encroachment on their habitat, combined with a low reproductive rate, rubber boas are deemed a species at risk. Consider yourself lucky if you see one, and observe from a distance.

↑ The rubber boa curls up in a ball when feeling threatened.

↖ The park has changed and grown since the 2003 wildfire.

Kalamalka Lake Provincial Park

This marl lake shines a brilliant blue-green in a dry grassland that showcases plenty of unique wildlife

What Makes This Hot Spot Hot?

- This park boasts a particularly large number of plant species, as well as a rare butterfly.
- Rattlesnakes may be seen during the warmer months after a long hibernation underground.
- Several stone artifacts remain in old village sites throughout the park that were traditionally used by the Okanagan First Nations.

Address: North Okanagan, BC (Parking is 10 km south of Vernon's city centre on Kidston Road)
Tel.: (250) 548-0076
Website: www.env.gov. bc.ca/bcparks/explore/ parkpgs/kalamalka_lk

GPS Coordinates
Latitude: 50.1858
Longitude: −119.24878

Open year-round

During the hot summer months Kalamalka Lake becomes a brilliant blue-green. Glaciers left behind deposits of limestone-rich mud, referred to as marlstone, and as the water warms during the summer the limestone crystals dissolve and reflect sunlight, giving the lake its turquoise colour.

The marl lake is surrounded by dry grasslands and stands of Douglas-fir and ponderosa pine. These trees have thick, fire resistant bark that allows them to stay alive in some forest fires. The dry grassland ecosystem is a haven for a number of rare and unique species, featuring many birds and over 400 plants. A unique insect to watch for is the immaculate green hairstreak — a small butterfly characterized by emerald-green wings dotted with a line of white spots. Look for its fuzzy, green caterpillar feeding on the yellow flowers of wild buckwheat.

The park is well known for its rattlesnake population. Although they are venomous, rattlesnakes will not bite unless they feel threatened. If you do happen to cross paths with one and can stay a couple metres away, have a look at its rattle. Snakes must shed their skin when they grow, and each time they

do so the snakes develop a new rattle segment, which they shake to warn people and other animals when they are too close. Detour around the snake, giving it a wide berth, and remember you are a visitor in its habitat. Proper footwear, such as boots that cover your ankles, is a good precaution to take while

hiking in this area. Kalamalka Lake is a beautiful and welcoming place for a swim on a hot summer's day at one of the designated swimming sites. In the winter cross-country skiers may enjoy the trails around the park. Although the paths are not groomed, they can make for a lovely day of skiing in the right conditions.

↑ This marl lake turns a beautiful shade of blue during the summer months.

↖ Visitors may see arrowleaf balsamroot blooming alongside the trails.

← If you are approaching a rattlesnake you will soon know it by the warning sound it makes with its rattle.

Knox Mountain

Friends of Knox Mountain advocate and practice stewardship, keeping the largest natural space in Kelowna visitor and wildlife friendly

What Makes This Hot Spot Hot?

- A spectacular array of flowers bloom in the spring and early summer.
- Visitors can drive, bike or hike to the top of Knox Mountain for beautiful views of the Okanagan Valley and the city of Kelowna.
- A variety of ecosystems within the park supports diverse wildlife close to Kelowna's downtown core.

Address: 450 Knox Mountain Drive, Kelowna, BC
Tel.: (250) 469-8800
Website: www.knoxmountainpark.ca

GPS Coordinates
Latitude: 49.9087
Longitude: −119.49159

Open year-round

↗ **The bitterroot flower blooms close to the ground.**

British Columbia usually evokes images of snow-peaked mountains and dense rainforests. However, the Okanagan and Similkameen valleys have something quite different to offer. At Knox Mountain, the largest natural space in Kelowna, an extensive trail system winds through a dry and delicate ecosystem composed of grasslands and pine and Douglas-fir trees. Just 3 kilometres north of downtown Kelowna, this park is an easily accessible natural oasis. For a space with so many visitors Knox Mountain is well preserved thanks to the Friends of Knox Mountain, who are in charge of the stewardship in the park.

During the spring and early summer months flowers bloom in the open, grassy fields. Dominated by arrowleaf balsamroot, arnica and brown-eyed Susan, the meadows are a charming display of green interlaced with striking yellow. Other flowers to look for include the purple mariposa lily and the pink bitterroot, which flowers low to the ground. Prickly pear cacti thrive in this environment and are well camouflaged on the dry ground.

Beginning on the shores of the Lake Okanagan, the park rises 300 metres to the top of Knox Mountain. On the trail to Paul's Tomb, which is a rocky beach, hikers will stay on a relatively flat trail that passes through grassy fields into a cooler pine and fir forest. The beach itself is a flat rocky bay, a lovely place for an afternoon swim. Alternatively, other trails or the paved road that takes you farther into the park bring you to the top of the mountain, where there is a mixture of grasslands, trees and marshes. There are multiple lookout points over Kelowna and the Okanagan Valley as you ascend. The park is frequented by local birders in search of songbirds, like the western bluebird, the chestnut-backed chickadee and the western meadowlark. You may also encounter a yellow-bellied marmot or mule deer grazing in the meadows.

↑ The view from Knox Mountain overlooking Kelowna.

→ The mariposa lily blooms early in the summer, adding a splash of purple to the grasslands.

LAC DU BOIS GRASSLANDS PROTECTED AREA

Mara Hill

Uniquely adapted flora and fauna call these dry grasslands home

What Makes This Hot Spot Hot?

- Hoodoos make a dramatic backdrop for this harsh environment.
- This area is home to several at-risk species, like the sharp-tailed grouse and western rattlesnake.
- There are opportunities for botanizing with many unique drought tolerant plants.

Address: Lac du Bois Grasslands Protected Area, Savona, BC
Tel.: (250) 371-6200
Website: www.env.gov. bc.ca/bcparks/explore/ parkpgs/lacdubois_grass

GPS Coordinates
Latitude: 50.73549
Longitude: −120.47313

Open year-round

↗ **The brittle prickly pear cactus can be found in the middle grasslands of Lac du Bois.**

→ **An artistic composition of lichens paints the landscape of Mara Hill.**

On the south end of the 15,712-hectare Lac du Bois Grasslands Protected Area, the picturesque Mara Hill stands out with striking geological formations. Exposed basalt has created spectacular cliffs, and sediments that were deposited by ancient lakes are now visible in the form of hoodoos along the lower slopes of Mara Hill. These pillars of weathered volcanic rock create a stunning backdrop for this ecologically diverse habitat.

Although the canyons, cliffs and open vistas of this area may seem void of life at first glance, there is much to be discovered. Grasslands provide habitat for 30 per cent of British Columbia's at-risk species, while making up only 1 per cent of the land base. These important areas support an abundance of wildlife and have been a key focus of conservation efforts for rare species, like the sharp-tailed grouse.

Just north of the railway tracks on Tranquille Road, Cinnamon Ridge Trail and Mara Trail are two of the most easily accessible hikes in the park. The trails provide excellent opportunities for viewing wildlife while admiring the unique geology of the area and the beautiful views of the surrounding grasslands. The trails in this area become more challenging as the elevation increases, so steady feet and good hiking shoes are required. In the hot summer months keep your eyes peeled

for the shy western rattle-snake, waiting out the sun to hunt in the cooler night.

The hot, dry climate leaves a harsh and delicate ecosystem with poor soil development, which makes for some unique local organisms. The bunchgrasses that cover the landscape are supported by a fragile layer of lichens, mosses and cyanobacteria. This cryptogamic crust helps retain moisture while stabilizing and fertilizing the soil. For this reason, it is critical that visitors stay on the trail.

Many plants here, like the big sagebrush, common rabbitbrush and prairie sagewort, have a distinct silvery look to them. This is due to tiny hairs covering their leaves, a trait that reduces water loss in this harsh climate. California bighorn sheep can often be seen on the slopes of Mara Hill or at nearby Dewdrop Cliffs. If you are lucky, you might be able to catch a glimpse of the blue-listed Lewis's woodpecker. This salmon-bellied bird may be seen behaving more like a flycatcher than a woodpecker as it captures meals on the wing.

↑ The release of iron from the volcanic rock gives Cinnamon Ridge its name, one of the amazing geological features of the beautiful and barren-looking grassland.

Mission Creek Greenway

A river runs through a variety of ecosystems that have many wildlife-viewing opportunities

What Makes This Hot Spot Hot?

- Meandering alongside Mission Creek in early September offers a chance to see kokanee salmon spawning.
- The calls of five different owl species may be heard during a night hike along this flat, easy trail.
- In the fall, leaves of deciduous trees create a colourful canopy and carpet the forest floor.

Address: Kelowna, BC
Tel.: (250) 763-4918
Website: www.regionaldistrict.com/your-services/parks-services/parks-and-trails/24-mission-creek-greenway.aspx

GPS Coordinates
Latitude: 49.87699
Longitude: −119.42705

Open year-round

Gaining momentum from a large watershed, Mission Creek moves through 43 kilometres of diverse ecosystems until it empties into Okanagan Lake. The Mission Creek Greenway is a trail system that runs alongside just over 15 kilometres of this waterway. This creek is an important breeding ground for the kokanee salmon, a landlocked species of sockeye salmon that spends its life in freshwater lakes. These fish were of great importance to the Okanagan First Nations, who would use the spawning season as an opportunity to harvest the fish, preserving them for the winter. In the 1950s the city dyked and altered the river in an attempt to reduce seasonal flooding. This caused the kokanee salmon population to plummet, which makes it all the more important for us to protect our watersheds from pollution.

The gravel walkway is largely shaded by deciduous trees that showcase their shades of orange, yellow and red leaves in the fall. The sight is so stunning that many Okanagan photographers choose this area as a location for engagement and other professional photo shoots.

As the greenway encompasses such a large area and so many habitats, it is an excellent place to spot a large variety of birds, particularly owls. Well hidden during the day five owl species, including the great horned owl, western screech owl and long-eared owl can all be found calling and hunting after dark.

At first glance the ground beneath the trees appears

↑ Many owls, including the great horned owl, call this riverside habitat home.

→ Any time of the year the Mission Greenway is a beautiful place for a riverside stroll through the forest.

↙ The mountain lady's slipper blooms in the early spring into the summer and grows in clusters near aspen trees.

to be made up of only grass, soil and the occasional shrub. However, if you look closer you will see that this is not the case. Inspect shaded areas near aspen trees to see the mountain lady's slipper alongside other flowers. As an orchid it is not surprising that this flower has such a unique structure, resembling a slipper. Orchids tend to evolve alongside pollinators, becoming very specific to the species that drink their nectar, and this particular orchid attracts small native bees.

SOUTH OKANAGAN GRASSLANDS AND PROTECTED AREA

Mount Kobau

At the top of a mountain in a desert lies a secluded haven for stargazers

What Makes This Hot Spot Hot?

- Stargazers can search the night sky for constellations from the top of a mountain at one of the premier stargazing spots in Canada.
- From a viewpoint small, coloured pools give Kliluk Lake a spotted appearance during the summer.
- Visitors can hike through a protected ecosystem inhabited by rare desert plants.

Address: South Okanagan Grasslands and Protected Area, Cawston, BC
Tel.: (1-800) 689-9025
Website: www.env.gov.bc.ca/bcparks/explore/parkpgs/s_ok_grassland

GPS Coordinates
Latitude: 49.11105
Longitude: −119.66694

Open year-round

↗ **The Brewer's sparrow is very well adapted to, and even dependant on, this ecosystem.**

One of four sites that compose the South Okanagan Grasslands Protected Area, Mount Kobau is well known as a stargazing destination. A drive or hike up the mountain gives visitors access to a panoramic view of the Okanagan Valley, which is beautiful both day and night. To protect the endangered ecosystem of dry grasslands this provincial park was established as a conservation area in 2001.

At night the vast sky is painted with stars, making Mount Kobau one of the best stargazing sites in Canada.

At the summit the sky is an uninterrupted canvas for starry nights. An annual stargazing event is held on the mountain summit every summer. There is a rough road through open pine forests and fields of desert flowers that ends in a parking lot close to the summit. From the parking lot walking trails meander around the mountain; an additional kilometre of established trail leads to the summit.

Bighorn sheep and sagebrush find protection here, but the park is also home to some of Canada's smaller treasures. Look closely at the

lichen coating trees and rocks and you may spot species that are new to scientists. One of the most impressive animals of the area is the Brewer's sparrow, a desert-adapted bird that can live for a week or more without a drink of water. These birds are dependant on the sagebrush for nesting habitat and materials, as well as a place to eat and sleep.

Although not technically in the protected area, Kliluk Lake, sometimes referred to as Spotted Lake, can be seen from the summit and is worth a closer look. During the summer much of the water in the lake evaporates. The mineral-rich lakebed is left with different coloured pools, which give the lake a unique spotted pattern. The lake was an important place of healing to the Okanagan First Nations.

↑ **The summit of Mount Kobau is a stargazer's dream.**

↓ **The nearby Kliluk Lake, or Spotted Lake, is famous for its mineral pools that give the lake its distinct pattern.**

Roderick Haig-Brown Provincial Park

Millions of sockeye salmon migrate back to the waters where they were born to start the life cycle once more

What Makes This Hot Spot Hot?

- The park is home to one of the largest sockeye salmon runs in North America.
- Every fourth year is a dominant run, when millions of salmon return to spawn.
- Important riparian habitat supports many species on land and in the water.

Address: 5 km north of Squilax on Squilax-Anglemont Road, BC
Tel.: (250) 955-0861
Website: www.env.gov. bc.ca/bcparks/explore/ parkpgs/roderick

GPS Coordinates
Latitude: 50.917833
Longitude: −119.625118

Open year-round

⛹ (Check ahead)

→ **Sockeye salmon travel the river to find an area with the right conditions, where each female lays thousands of eggs.**

There are many notable rivers to view the spectacular salmon runs that occur throughout British Columbia, but the Adams River hosts one of the most impressive. A trip to Roderick Haig-Brown Provincial Park in the fall provides opportunities to see multiple species of salmon travelling up the river to spawn, including coho, pink and chinook varieties. The truly astounding event, however, is the sockeye run.

The most famous and brilliantly coloured salmon species in BC, sockeye return to the Adams River to spawn in the same fresh waters they were born. Retracing the path they navigated to reach the ocean years earlier, these salmon travel thousands of kilometres to the alluvial gravel riverbeds of this area, which creates an ideal habitat for developing salmon.

Although some sockeye return to the river each

year, every fourth year is a dominant year, and the number of returning salmon is staggering. This four-year pattern is thanks to a phenomenon called cyclic dominance, where most offspring produced in any one brood return to spawn four years later, although they may be mature anywhere between the ages of 2 and 6 years old. The next major spawning run is anticipated for 2018, but the subdominant run the year following each dominant run is still exciting, with hundreds of thousands of salmon returning to these waters.

While the salmon spectacle is definitely a must-see, Roderick Haig Brown Provincial Park is an excellent place to visit any time of year, with 26 kilometres of trails to explore. The park protects 11 kilometres of critically important habitat along the riverbank, and the dying bodies of the mated salmon replenish the system and provide vital nutrients to support the surrounding terrestrial ecosystem. During dominant years, visit the park in the first three weeks of October to witness the sockeye spawning; other species of salmon can be seen spawning slightly earlier in the season. A large viewing platform offers a prime spot to watch, as the salmon search for the perfect place to lay their eggs.

↑ Spawning male sockeye salmon develop a brilliant red body, humped back, green head and hooked beak.

↓ Bald eagles visit the river during the spawning season for a fishy feast.

Skaha Bluffs Provincial Park

Towering cliffs and shaded valleys provide important habitat for animals big and small

What Makes This Hot Spot Hot?

- The park is a protected area and important migration corridor for bighorn sheep.
- Visitors can take in panoramic views of Skaha Lake and the city of Penticton atop rocky bluffs.
- This is a geological paradise that is ideal for cliff-dwelling birds and bats.

Address: Smythe Drive, Penticton, BC
Tel.: (250) 548-0076
Website: www.env.gov. bc.ca/bcparks/explore/ parkpgs/skahaBluffs

GPS Coordinates
Latitude: 49.4307
Longitude: –119.56393

Open March 1 to November 15

→ **Forests and grasslands surrounded by rocky cliffs are characteristic of Skaha.**

Named for the rocky bluffs that define the surrounding landscape, Skaha Bluffs Provincial Park is a place of geological interest to naturalists and rock climbers from around the world. Visitors can walk on a trail system that passes through valleys carved by the ebb and flow of glaciers and gaze upon rocky outcrops that provide habitat to a variety of birds as well as four bat species. White-throated swifts dart in and out of rock cavities, and the call of the western screech owl echoes through the canyons. Particularly well adapted to this environment is the canyon wren. With a low centre of gravity and large feet, this songbird scales rock faces with ease, thrusting its narrow head into rock holes as it forages for insects.

From the parking lot, the park's trails move through dry grasslands with shallow, rocky soil and pine forests. If you are lucky you may see bighorn sheep grazing in the grasslands. This is an important protected habitat for these aptly named sheep — their

horns can weigh up to 14 kilograms. Also keep an eye out for western rattlesnakes basking on sun-heated rocks. A blotchy, brown snake with a large triangular head, this species is easily recognizable by the rattle on its tail. Each time a rattlesnake sheds its skin a new segment of its rattle is produced. Rattlesnakes are not aggressive and will only bite in defense. If you do see one remember you are in its home. Give it space and either backtrack

→ The canyon wren is well adapted to canyon life.

⌄ The park provides important habitat for bighorn sheep.

or go around it if possible.

As the trails make their way into the park's shaded valleys, the vegetation changes dramatically. An abundance of greenery surrounds the low points of the valley where water gathers. This habitat is ideal for the Pacific chorus frog. Although it can be found quite far from water, it relies on small pools for breeding. Look for this small, bright-green frog on the ground or climbing up short plants.

sẁiẁs Provincial Park

Previously known as Haynes Point, this park protects many rare amphibian, plant and bird species

What Makes This Hot Spot Hot?

- The park is located on a peninsula that connects to a sandbar, which creates a land bridge and makes the lake crossable by foot.
- The calliope hummingbird, Canada's smallest hummingbird, calls this park home.
- Unique hardy plants thrive in the dry, desert-like conditions of this park.

Address: 32nd Avenue, Osoyoos, BC
Tel.: (778) 437-2295
Website: www.env.gov.bc.ca/bcparks/explore/parkpgs/swiws

GPS Coordinates
Latitude: 49.01483
Longitude: –119.45769

Open year-round

⤴ **The calliope hummingbird is the smallest hummingbird in Canada.**

Upon the discovery of an important archaeological site containing the remains of the Osoyoos Indian Band's Okanagan ancestors, management of this provincial park was handed from BC Parks to the Osoyoos Indian Band. The name was changed from Haynes Point to sẁiẁs Provincial Park, the Okanagan First Peoples' name for the area. Sẁiẁs, pronounced "s-wee-yous" and meaning "a shallow or narrow place in the middle of a lake," refers to the traditional crossing point of Osoyoos Lake by foot or on horseback. The park is situated on a peninsula that extends almost completely across the lake. The tip of the peninsula meets a shallow sandbar that continues to the other side.

Sẁiẁs Park is a popular site for birders, plant enthusiasts and those interested in herpetology, the study of amphibians and reptiles. Containing dry grasslands, this small desert park attracts flocks of lakeshore and marshland birds. Alongside marsh wrens, yellow-headed blackbirds and families of

quails, Canada's smallest hummingbird, the calliope hummingbird, calls this park home. They may be small, but the bright purple throat is difficult to miss. Lookout towers and benches along the 2-kilometre trail ensure many opportunities to view wildlife.

A marshy haven within the dry desert, this park was initially established in an effort to protect its desert plants. Species such as bushy cinquefoil, awned cyperus and peach leaf willow flourish in this environment. Alongside these plants, the park also provides refuge to a number of endangered animals, such as the blotched tiger salamander. Although this red-listed amphibian spends much of its life seeking shade in underground burrows or beneath stumps, it is sometimes seen by lucky visitors. Painted turtles are much less elusive, openly sunbathing on logs in the marsh. As you walk the trails, tread lightly and look for the spadefoot toad before it burrows into the mud with its spade-shaped hind legs. The amount of amphibian and aquatic reptile species supported by this otherwise dry environment speaks to the park's continued importance as a protected area.

↑ The spadefoot toad is one of the amphibians found in the wetlands of the park.

↖ The peninsula on which the park sits spans nearly the entire width of Osoyoos Lake.

UBC Okanagan Trails

This trail system is an excellent example of how a university can incorporate green spaces for all

What Makes This Hot Spot Hot?

- From early morning bird walks to a stroll through the forest or alongside a pond, these trails have plenty to enjoy.
- The trails offer an immersive natural experience on a university campus and close to the city of Kelowna.
- Approximately 170 species of plants and animals exist on and around the trails.

Address: 3333 University Way, Kelowna, BC
Tel.: (250) 807-8000
Website: maps.ok.ubc.ca/map

GPS Coordinates
Latitude: 49.93986
Longitude: −119.39671

Open year-round

↗ **Western bluebirds enjoy the open spaces in nearby fields.**

Their ease of access and wild biodiversity make the UBC Okanagan Trails a joy for Kelowna locals. The trails may be on the University of British Columbia's Okanagan campus, but the university welcomes the sensitive use and enjoyment of its campus trail system by Okanagan residents as well as visitors. Although the trails are less than 2 kilometres long, they meander through a wide variety of habitats.

The Old Pond Trail, which loops around a gorgeous little pond teeming with life, is just steps off a paved road. Once you hear the red-winged blackbirds start calling through the reeds that line the pond's edge, it is easy to feel immersed in nature. In the evening great horned owls can be heard from the trees, and bats swoop down to drink from the pond before their nightly hunt for insects.

North of the campus the Pine Trail loop takes off into the forest and is connected

to the Old Pond Trail by the Juniper Trail. The Pine Trail borders green spaces and connects to trails around Robert Lake. The trail is also a sanctuary for early morning birding and afternoon strolls. Pine siskins and downy woodpeckers, among other birds, can be heard calling in the forest. Bring binoculars to gaze at the bordering fields where western bluebirds are often perched along fences.

Insects are found during the warmer months on any of the trails. Mourning cloak butterflies, with their brown wings with white and blue markings, and cabbage white butterflies may be seen fluttering about. Look closely at the trees and ground and you will see many species of lichen, fungi and moss in this pine forest. In a 2015 survey

of the area, 170 species were found on and around these trails. The campus is easily accessible by bus, but if you are driving, note that paid parking is in effect 24 hours.

↑ Listen for the call of birds in the dry pine forests.

↖ The Old Pond Trail, a short walk from the bustling campus, feels secluded and hosts many plants and animals.

182

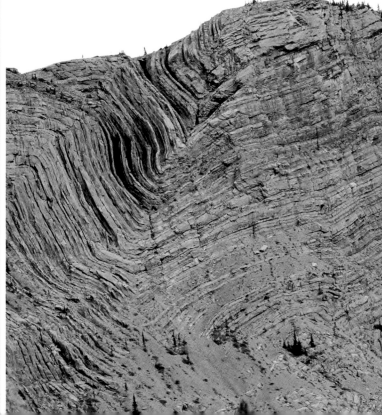

Northern British Columbia

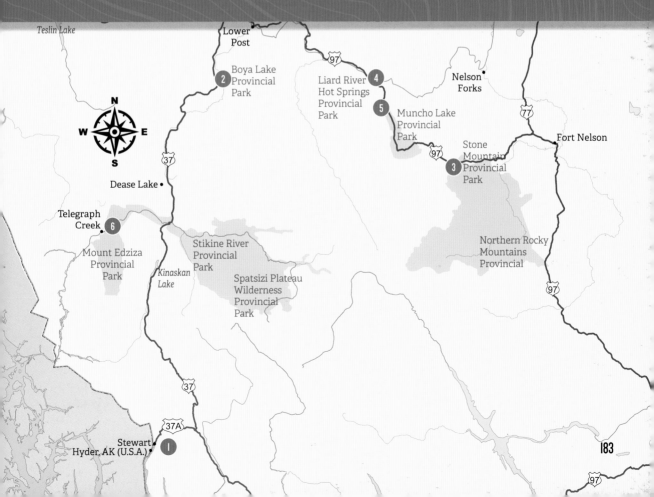

Teslin Lake

Lower Post

2 Boya Lake Provincial Park

Liard River Hot Springs Provincial Park 4

5 Muncho Lake Provincial Park

Nelson Forks

97

77

Fort Nelson

37

Stone Mountain Provincial Park 3

97

Dease Lake

Telegraph Creek 6

Mount Edziza Provincial Park

Kinaskan Lake

Stikine River Provincial Park

Spatsizi Plateau Wilderness Provincial Park

Northern Rocky Mountains Provincial

97

37

37A

Stewart
Hyder, AK (U.S.A.) 1

97

97

Bear and Salmon Glaciers

The glaciers are all on BC soil, but you will need your passport to make the most of these breathtaking views

What Makes This Hot Spot Hot?

- Views of beautiful glaciers and waterfalls are all along the drive into Stewart.
- Salmon Glacier is the fifth largest glacier in Canada.
- Marmots and other wildlife can be seen from the road and lookouts.

Address: Glacier Hwy (Stewart Hwy or Hwy 37A), Stewart, BC
Tel.: N/A
Websites: www.env.gov.bc.ca/bcparks/explore/parkpgs/bear_gl, www.stewartcassiarhighway.com/attractions/salmon-glacier

GPS Coordinates
Latitude: 56.097455
Longitude: −129.667406

Open year-round, conditions permitting

The drive along the appropriately named Glacier Highway (also known as Stewart Highway or Highway 37A) into the small town of Stewart is one of the most picturesque drives in the province, with spectacular views around every corner. There are many pull-offs along the road to support the nature lover's desire to stop and admire the dramatic surroundings as the drive takes you past many glaciers, mountain waterfalls, rushing rivers, rolling streams and steep rock walls. Watch for wildlife on the road, as black bears and grizzlies are found in the area, and there is opportunity for roadside birding. Listen for the short, burry calls of the western tanager for a chance to catch a glimpse of this shy yet lavishly coloured bird.

Glaciers often appear blue, simply because, just as in large bodies of water, the molecules in these massive pieces of compressed ice absorb other colours of light more efficiently than blue. The pressure that creates such a dense piece of ice also squeezes out air bubbles that would otherwise make the ice appear white.

The most famous ice formation along this stretch of highway is the Bear Glacier, protected within provincial parkland. Although it once completely filled the Bear River Pass, the glacier began to retreat in the 1940s, and where once was ice, now a lake has formed. Although the beautiful glacial tongue is still an awe-inspiring roadside stop, it is worth looking for evidence in the rocks and slopes of its once grander size. This rapidly shrinking glacier is a startling reminder that glacial retreats are among the most dramatic indicators of climate change.

Bring your passport with you on this trip, because once in Stewart, a worthwhile crossing through American soil will bring you back across the border into BC to admire the magnificent Salmon Glacier. The drive takes you through the Alaskan ghost town of Hyder, where the only customs you will encounter is when you re-enter Canada. The 37-kilometre drive to the lookout over the glacier

provides additional wildlife viewing opportunities. You will have a good chance of seeing hoary marmots along the way between May and August, the only months of the year they are not hibernating. Marmots thrive in rocky alpine terrain, hiding from predators in burrows. In the summer you may see moms feeding and sunbathing with their babies, who stay with them for two years before venturing off on their own.

Salmon Glacier, found just on the Canadian side of the border, is the fifth largest glacier in the country. From the viewpoint you can see

where the enormous ice field splits into two tongues. Look for terminal moraines near the glacial toe, where sediments scraped and carried by the river of ice are deposited.

↑ Views of the massive Salmon Glacier are worth the trek through American soil.

↖ Meltwater rushes down from the toe of Bear Glacier.

Boya Lake Provincial Park

A paradise lake nestled in the boreal forest that feigns a tropical destination

What Makes This Hot Spot Hot?

- The lake's marl bottom results in brilliant turquoise hues.
- The complex lake system is a perfect opportunity for exploration by canoe or kayak.
- A beautiful trail leads to an active beaver lodge.

Address: Liard Plain, Stikine Region, BC
Tel.: (250) 638-8490
Website: www.env.gov. bc.ca/bcparks/explore/ parkpgs/boya_lk

GPS Coordinates
Latitude: 59.368496
Longitude: −129.108686

Open May to September

♿ (Check ahead)

↗ **A beaver heads back to the shore in search of suitable branches.**

When you first arrive at the water's edge of Boya Lake you might need to pinch yourself to be sure you have not been transported to the Caribbean. This lake's stunning aquamarine colour is thanks to its marl bottom, consisting of a mixture of silt and shell fragments. The colour reflecting from the bottom through crystal-clear waters makes for a striking, almost tropical scene, although a scan of the trees, wildflowers and snow-capped peaks will bring you back to northern British Columbia's beautiful Liard Plain landscape.

The body of water you see from the campground and day-use area comprises only a small portion of the total area of the lake. Made up of many islands, complex winding inlets and channels, and other smaller bodies of water cut off from the main lake, the lake's convoluted characteristics make it the perfect park for exploring by canoe or kayak. If you do not have your own, it is possible to rent one from the BC Parks Area Supervisor on site. As this is one of the few lakes in this area of the province that is warm enough to swim in, be sure to come prepared for some water exploration.

Boya Lake has two short hiking trails that are each worth exploring. The Lakeshore Trail loop, accessed from the north end of the campground, provides additional views of winding shoreline and radiant water. From the south end of the day-use area

of Canada's hardworking celebrity species, the North American beaver. As beavers drag branches and logs from the shoreline to their dams or lodges, dirt and debris mix in with the marl bottom. A viewing platform is set up for watching these beavers at work. Keep an eye out for them as they travel back and forth to pick up branches either for immediate consumption or to store for the winter ahead. If they notice you watching they may perform one of their signature behaviours — giving each other warnings by slapping their fat, leathery tails on the surface of the water.

a trail leads along an esker before retreating back down to the water. You may notice the water is less clear and blue in this area of the park, thanks to the tireless work

↑ On a sunny day Boya Lake gives the impression of a more tropical paradise.

← A woodpecker cavity and bear-claw scars show that beavers are not the only animals making use of the nearby trees.

STONE MOUNTAIN PROVINCIAL PARK

Flower Springs Lake Trail

Alpine meadows contrasted with stark mountain views

What Makes This Hot Spot Hot?

- This area provides habitat for woodland caribou and other large mammals.
- Diverse wildflowers blanket the alpine meadows.
- The end of the trail is marked by a large glacial lake nestled at the bottom of Mount Saint George.

Address: Summit Lake Campground, Stone Mountain Provincial Park, Alaska Hwy (Hwy 97), Northern Rockies B, BC
Tel.: (250) 776-7000
Websites: www.env.gov.bc.ca/bcparks/explore/parkpgs/stone_mt, www.northernrockies.ca/assets/Visitors/PDFs/FlowerSprings.pdf

GPS Coordinates
Latitude: 58.651457
Longitude: –124.648311

Open May to mid-September (the park closes when snow falls)

↗ **A male woodland caribou with his velvety antlers.**

Giant masses of exposed stone mountains rise from green valleys, making Stone Mountain Provincial Park a must-see destination in northeastern British Columbia. The park lies largely within the alpine tundra geoclimatic zone, so trees are already sparse even before you begin hiking farther up into the alpine meadows. Summit Lake Campground in the park is one of the most exposed campgrounds in the entire province, sitting about 1,270 metres above sea level, so if you are planning on camping, be prepared for a windy night.

For experienced backpackers, there are plenty of opportunities for backcountry exploration, but the park also offers several day-hikes to fantastic views of alpine meadows and glacial lakes. The Flower Springs Lake Trail comprises two routes: the lake edge route is a 13.6-kilometre return hike to a lovely lake at the base of Mount Saint George, and the radio tower route is a 10.2-kilometre return hike that follows a radio tower road. The second route is shorter and provides a more gradual ascent for the first half of the hike. The trail traverses through moist, flooded land as it traces the North Tetsa River but quickly climbs into more exposed meadow.

As you gain elevation throughout the hike, trees become more and more sparse, but the early summer wildflowers continue to impress, adding splashes of colour to the green meadows. Mountain lupines, white mountain-heather, field locoweed, mountain monkshood, shooting star, narcissus anemone and moss campion are highlights along the trail.

During dawn and dusk, woodland caribou are known to visit Flower Springs Lake. Unique to the deer family, both male and female caribou grow antlers, although some females only grow one, and others none at all. Caribou are also special in that their winter diet is almost exclusively lichens, which is the reason for their winter migration into coniferous forests. Their wide hooves act as snowshoes in deep snow and also help them dig out lichens. In the summer they spend most of their time in the alpine regions, where snow patches provide refuge from the heat and biting insects.

The park is home to other large mammals, so look out for mountain goats, moose, black bears and grizzly bears. Smaller mammal species live in the park as well, including dusky shrews, porcupines, least chipmunks and several species of vole. Pack your binoculars and be on the lookout for boreal chickadees, American tree sparrows and American pipits, which can be spotted bobbing their tails in the open meadows near the glacial lake.

↑ The bright blue water, bright green meadow and light-grey mountains provide a picture-perfect backdrop to this hike.

↓ White mountain-heather form dense mats along the trail.

Liard River Hot Springs Provincial Park

Exceptional and provincially unique organisms call these hot waters home

What Makes This Hot Spot Hot?

- This is the only place in the world where you can find hotwater physa snails.
- Species found way outside their normal range thrive in the warm waters here.
- Wood bison are locally abundant within the park and easy to spot from the road.

Address: 497 Alaska Hwy (Hwy 97), Muncho Lake, BC
Tel.: (250) 776-7000
Website: www.env.gov.
bc.ca/bcparks/explore/
parkpgs/liard_rv_hs

GPS Coordinates
Latitude: 59.419877
Longitude: −126.089826

Open year-round

♿ (Check ahead)

Like many hot springs scattered across the province, Liard River Hot Springs Provincial Park is a popular destination for those looking for a tranquil and steaming dip in natural waters. However, these springs are unlike any other in the province and are home to species found nowhere else in the world. As a general rule, hot springs are brimming with specialized organisms that are able to make a living in these unusual and harsh conditions. These hot springs take it one step further, providing refuge to some rare species, even by hot spring standards.

The Liard River system has at least six hot springs feeding into pools and streams that eventually drain into a marsh. As hot water flows into shallower areas farther from the source, it cools off, depositing calcium carbonate that was picked up as the water moved through underground limestone deposits. The carbonate minerals from the water harden to form deposits of tufa, a type of limestone. Chara, thought to be a late common ancestor of algae and land plants, becomes encrusted in the calcium carbonate and provides a habitat for Liard River's rarest animals.

The hotwater physa is a tiny freshwater snail found here and nowhere else in the world. The snails thrive in waters between 23 and 40 degrees Celsius, feeding on organisms that live on the chara's crusty surface. Between 3 and 9 millimetres in length, this tiny mollusc needs the support of the park's visitors to ensure its survival, or else it faces global extinction. Do not disturb the sensitive habitat in the marsh, as the wide boardwalk provides fabulous viewing opportunities in this unique environment without having to touch anything. The use of all soaps, oils, sunscreens and other skin products by bathers

is prohibited in the springs upstream to protect this spectacular nature hot spot.

Other provincially rare natives to the marsh are thankfully much easier to spot than the miniscule physas. A population of lake chub is found here, able to tolerate the high temperatures. Look for this small, well-camouflaged fish darting around in small clearings in the marshy water surrounding the boardwalk. The plains forktail, a dainty damselfly typically found in the most southern reaches of Canada's prairies, can be spotted along the boardwalk. Unique populations like these are probably relicts of warmer days: during a warming after the retreat of the glaciers that once covered the province, these species were likely more widespread, but their range is now constrained to the hot springs.

Liard River Hot Springs Provincial Park is also home to some impressive large mammals, including moose, which are sometimes seen visiting the warm marsh waters. In the forests surrounding the hot springs, the Nahanni population of wood bison is locally abundant. Watch for the hefty solitary males, who may weigh up to 900 kilograms, feeding or resting in clearings beside the highway, as well as large herds of females and their calves, often accompanied by yearlings and a few bulls. As North America's largest land mammals, wood bison are hard to miss, and these imposing giants are certainly not shy, requiring traffic to yield to them, and not vice versa.

↑ A raised boardwalk takes you up to the Hanging Garden, where tufa creates a terraced base for plants to grow.

↓ A wood bison calf makes for a memorable wildlife sighting in this provincial park.

Muncho Lake Provincial Park

Abundant spring wildflowers, a beautiful jade-green lake and fantastic wildlife-viewing opportunities

What Makes This Hot Spot Hot?

- Stone's sheep are often seen in the park, licking mineral deposits.
- The distinct rock layers visible in Folded Mountain showcase the origins of mountain formation.
- Wildflowers are a park highlight in the spring and early summer, easily found along the park trails.

Address: Muncho Lake, BC
Tel.: (250) 776-7000
Website: www.env.gov. bc.ca/bcparks/explore/ parkpgs/muncho_lk

GPS Coordinates
Latitude: 58.994106
Longitude: –125.763332

Open year-round

 (Check ahead)

↗ **The delicate flower of the unassuming common butterwort reveals nothing of its carnivorous tendencies.**

Muncho Lake Provincial Park offers great opportunities for camping on the water, where you will fall asleep to the enchanting tremolo call of the common loon echoing across the jade-green lake. The park has much to offer outside of lake views, however, with something for everyone — especially botany, zoology and geology enthusiasts.

Visible from the Alaska Highway (Highway 97), which cuts through the park, Folded Mountain provides a picture-perfect snapshot into how these mountains came to be. For over a billion years, the land that now makes up the mountains of the region was a shallow seabed that, accumulating layer after layer, ultimately formed sedimentary rock. Since then the land has been transformed as tectonic plates shifted and collided, forcing the once-horizontal rock layers to buckle and fold, now clearly revealed in the patterns of Folded Mountain.

Limestone, dolomite and shale were carved from the mountains by ancient glaciers, creating a fine rock flour. These mineral deposits are important for hoofed mammals that require the elements present in the rock flour for their tooth, hair and bone growth. As a result, these animals travel many kilometres to access these mineral licks. Stone's sheep, a subspecies of the thinhorn sheep, visit the licks often in the spring and early summer, but you may also spot this agile mammal along the roadside and hiking trails in the area.

The trail at the Mineral Licks Viewing Area, marked from the highway, is a 1.5-kilometre loop that provides a

good chance to see Stone's sheep and other ungulates, as well as offers fabulous wildflower viewing along the trail. In the spring and early summer be on the lookout for common butterwort. This small, unassuming herb, with its single violet, funnel-shaped flower, is surprisingly a carnivorous plant. Look closely at the chartreuse basal leaves, and you may notice insects that have fallen victim to this plant's unique adaptation. The upper surface of the leaves creates a greasy secretion to trap its food, and the rolled edges prevent prey from escaping along the leaf perimeter. Trapped insects, which are slowly digested by enzymes secreted by the plant, help it survive in nutrient-poor soils.

↑ Small groups of Stone's sheep may be spotted along open slopes throughout the park.

↖ Folded Mountain reveals its geological history in waved layers of sedimentary rock.

Stikine River Canyon

Eighty kilometres of steep-walled canyon are unlike anything else in Canada

What Makes This Hot Spot Hot?

- Sometimes referred to as the Grand Canyon of the Stikine, the canyon has walls that rise 300 metres from the raging river below.
- The chasm ranges from 200 metres to as little as 2 metres wide.
- Bank swallows nest along the sandy banks of the roadside en route to canyon views.

Address: Telegraph Creek Road, Telegraph Creek, BC
Tel.: N/A
Website: www.env.gov. bc.ca/bcparks/explore/ parkpgs/stikine

GPS Coordinates
Latitude: 58.013252
Longitude: −130.977095

Open year-round, conditions permitting

↗ **You can find large numbers of bank swallows nesting in the soft, sandy substrate along the road.**

Eighty kilometres of steep-walled canyons rise up from the raging waters of the Stikine River, which carved away at the basalt and sedimentary rock over great expanses of time to create the dramatic vista you see now. This impressive river, which passes through Stikine River Provincial Park and traces the northern edge of Mount Edziza Provincial Park, becomes impassable as it flows through the canyon, making exploration on water only possible in the Upper Stikine.

The drive to the canyon is not for the faint of heart — much of Telegraph Creek Road on this 110-kilometre journey from Dease Lake is narrow, winding and steep, including grades up to 20 per cent as the road crosses water where the Tuya River meets the Stikine. There are no shoulders, few signs and no facilities along the way, so plan ahead and know what you are getting into before committing to the journey. That said, for those willing to make the drive, the views are fabulous. There is a pull-off with a great view of the Stikine Canyon without

having to go all the way into the town of Telegraph Creek. You can also look out over the Tuya River earlier on the drive near the northern edge of the park border. Although expensive, plane and helicopter flights over the canyon are available and would make for a once-in-a-lifetime experience. If you visit in the autumn, the fall colours alongside the steep canyons look incredible.

More than 300 mountain goats call this canyon home, using the steep cliffsides as an escape route from their predators, so look for white dots perched on distant cliffs when you stop to admire the canyon. You will pass a large colony of bank swallows on your drive

through the park, thankfully along a stretch with enough space to pull over and admire these acrobatic birds. The quick, fluttering movements of these small swallows are a sight to see, as they swoop around each other in the air, catching insects on the wing.

Right next to the road, in the high vertical sandy banks, are a large group of nesting holes. These nest chambers are dug out by the male bank swallows using their feet, wings and conical bills. They burrow about a metre straight into the bank!

↑ **A lookout reveals the near vertical drop from the top of the canyon to the rushing river below.**

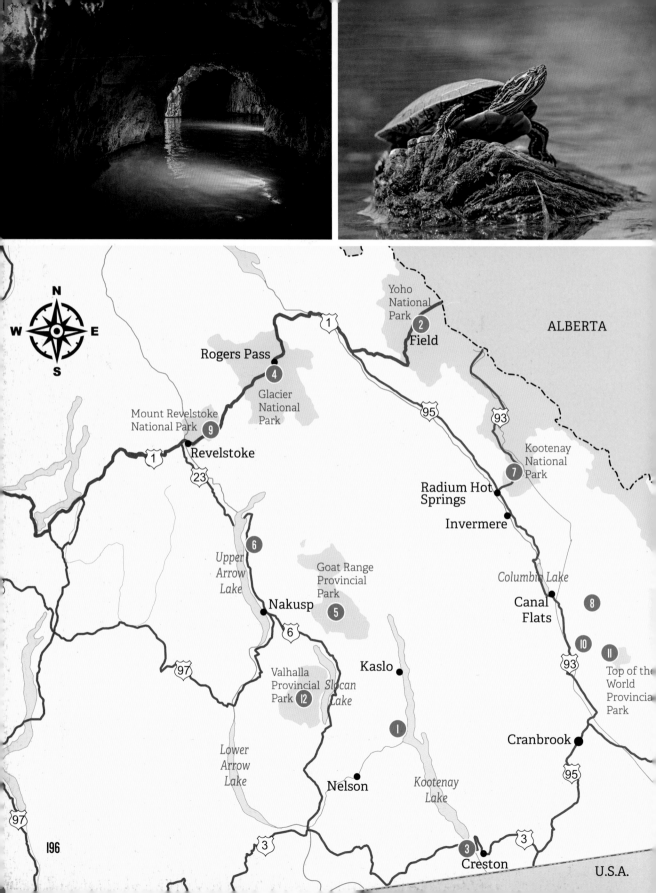

ALBERTA

Yoho National Park
② Field

Rogers Pass
④
Glacier National Park

Mount Revelstoke National Park
⑨
① Revelstoke
23

95

93

Kootenay National Park
⑦

Radium Hot Springs
Invermere

⑥
Upper Arrow Lake

Goat Range Provincial Park
⑤

Nakusp
6

97

Columbia Lake
Canal Flats
⑧

Kaslo

Valhalla Provincial Park
⑫ Slocan Lake

①
⑩ 93
⑪
Top of the World Provincial Park

Lower Arrow Lake

Cranbrook

Nelson
Kootenay Lake

95

97

3
3

196

③
Creston

U.S.A.

The Kootenay Region

Ainsworth Hot Springs

A must-do hot spring in the Kootenays and a swim through a uniquely shaped limestone cave

What Makes This Hot Spot Hot?

- Visitors can relax in two developed mineral hot springs and take a quick dip in a cold pool.
- Steaming water seeps out of the rock, flowing into a horseshoe-shaped cave where it creates a natural sauna.
- The nearby Cody Caves, carved out of limestone and filled with magnificent cave features, are the origins of the hot spring's waters.

Address: 3609 Balfour-Kaslo-Galena Bay Hwy (Hwy 31), BC
Tel.: (1-800) 668-1171
Website: www.ainsworthhotsprings.com

GPS Coordinates
Latitude: 49.73574
Longitude: −116.91131

Open year-round

↗**Steaming water seeps out of the rock into a horseshoe-shaped cave.**

With hot springs and scenic views, this hot spot is well known as a place to relax. The Ainsworth Hot Springs were used by the Ktunaxa First Nation as a place of healing and are traditionally called *nupika wu'u*, which translates to "spirit water." The developed hot springs are famous for their cave-swimming feature. In its natural state the cave was over 2 metres long but has since been carved into a 46-metre horseshoe in which visitors can float and wade.

Near the back of the cave hot water flows out of the rock and into the pool. The water goes on quite the underground journey before ending up in these springs. Starting in the nearby Cody Caves, the water flows underground through cracks in the bedrock, gradually increasing in temperature. When it eventually reaches Kootenay Lake it is forced upwards and flows out of the rock, filling the pools with steaming water.

To see the origins of these waters as well as stunning limestone cave formations, be sure to visit Cody Caves. From here the water is pulled underground and completely refills the hot springs up to six times each day! To experience the

surrounding wildlife and landscapes, enjoy a day of hiking in the nearby town of Kaslo, which has a number of hikes, including to Mount Buchanan, a lovely trail through mountain meadows leading to a lookout over Kootenay Lake. The Wagon Road Trail is great for a stroll through the forest to Fish Lake, where hikers will see swallowtail butterflies fluttering alongside other insects, all of which attract a wide variety of insect-eating birds. Look for the brightly coloured yellow warbler chirping as it darts between the trees. On the lakes a variety of ducks, including the goldeneye, is a common sight. A soak in the hot springs with a beautiful view over Kootenay Lake will be particularly relaxing after a day of hiking and wildlife watching.

As Ainsworth Hot Springs are a developed resort there is an entry fee to access them. As well, Cody Caves have only guided tours to protect the caves' delicate features.

↑ **Hike the trails of the nearby community of Kaslo for wildlife watching opportunities.**

YOHO NATIONAL PARK

Burgess Shale

These rocky slopes protect some of the world's most important fossils

What Makes This Hot Spot Hot?

- There are opportunities to learn about the origins of modern plant and animal life while looking at fossils, some of which could be distant ancestors of humans.
- Amazingly detailed fossils preserved from the Cambrian explosion give a glimpse into life over 500 million years ago.
- Visitors can enjoy interpretive tours of two important fossil sites while hiking in the Rocky Mountains.

Address: Field, BC
Tel.: (1-800) 343-3006 (Burgess Shale Geoscience Foundation) or (1-877) 737-3783 (Parks Canada)
Websites: www.burgess-shale. bc.ca, www.pc.gc.ca/en/pn-np/bc/yoho/activ/burgess

GPS Coordinates
Latitude: 51.39686
Longitude: –116.48698

Open mid-June through mid-September when guided hikes are available, conditions permitting

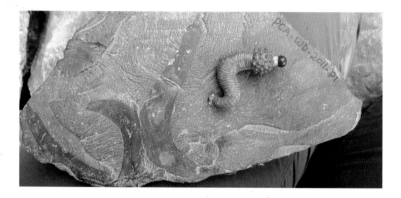

↑ **Scientists were able to create a model of animals such as the Ottoia, a completely soft-bodied creature, from these well-preserved fossils.**

In Yoho National Park, visitors can see some of the most important fossil beds in the world. The remnants of marine life from 505 million years ago are preserved in the alpine of the Rocky Mountains.

There are two sites to visit in the park, each a rewarding hike with views of the Rockies. The fossilized creatures at these sites give us a glimpse into the Cambrian period, when the first complex animals and ecosystems appeared in the fossil record. Truly representing an explosion of life, some 120 animal fossils found in the Burgess Shale fit into phyla (a classification of living things) that we did not know existed.

Mount Stephen was the first site to be discovered in 1886 following reports of "stone bugs" being found by railway workers. The tour to the site is a steep but manageable 8-kilometre hike to an abundance of fossils, including many trilobites, which are ancient and extinct arthropods.

In 1909 Charles Walcott, a paleontologist and the leading expert on Cambrian fossils at the time, happened upon a fossil of *Marrella splendens* alongside a trail. With its long head spikes, Marrella is thought to be an ancestor of many modern arthropods, such as crustaceans and arachnids. After following a

path of shale debris up the rocky slope, Walcott discovered what would later be called the Walcott Quarry. The renowned Walcott Quarry tour is a 22-kilometre round trip. The fossils at this quarry are so well preserved that soft body parts are identifiable and can even show who ate who in this ancient ecosystem. A once-bustling ocean saw a sudden landslide of sediment, which created an environment low in oxygen that turned out to be perfect for preserving creatures with mostly or entirely soft bodies, including ancient sponges and worms.

To protect the delicate nature of the sites, visitors require guides. Both the Burgess Shale Geoscience Foundation and Parks Canada offer excellent interpretive tours in which you are able to get up close and learn about many of the fossils. At the quarries guides talk about the fossils and pass around spectacular examples of each, and then visitors are allowed time to explore the shale themselves. Nearly every overturned rock reveals another fossil.

↑ A charming view of Emerald Lake from the Walcott Quarry.

↓ The hike to the Walcott Quarry includes trails through alpine meadows.

Creston Valley Wildlife Management Area

These wetlands are British Columbia's most important inland habitat for migratory birds

What Makes This Hot Spot Hot?

- Nearly 400 species of birds, mammals and amphibians use these wetlands as a home or stopover during migration.
- Ongoing research and active wetland management ensure the continued health of the wetlands and the species that call them home.
- These wetlands provide flood control for the surrounding area.

Address: 1760 West Creston Road, Creston, BC
Tel.: (250) 402-6900
Website: www.crestonwildlife.ca

GPS Coordinates
Latitude: 49.12105
Longitude: –116.63496

Open year-round

Water spills from the nearby Kootenay River into Duck Lake and its surrounding wetlands, creating a paradise for wildlife. Recognized as a Ramsar Wetland of International Importance and an Important Bird Area, these lakes and marshes are protected and thriving.

The year-round biodiversity supported by these wetlands is impressive. Many species of amphibians, mammals and birds frequent the area. Moose and species at risk such as the western painted turtle are not uncommon sights. Both the northern leopard frog and Forster's tern have chosen this site to host their only breeding populations in British Columbia.

These wetlands are considered the most important inland area for migrating birds, allowing them to rest, feed and nest. The area supports many plants used by birds as materials for making nests, which are very diverse

↑ **Osprey use large sticks to build their nests high up in trees or atop human-made structures.**

↓ **The northern leopard frog calls these wetlands home.**

among species. Songbirds will often weave delicate nests out of grasses, sometimes incorporating snakeskins. Tundra swans pile a variety of grasses and twigs over natural features on the ground. Nuthatches will nest in hollows

→ **A paddle through the wetlands reveals a unique perspective.**

in trees, and some birds, such as the osprey, make messy-looking nests by piling large sticks high up in tall trees. Plastics and other garbage can sometimes be mistaken by birds as nest-building material. That is why the conservation and protection of this area during nesting season are of particular importance.

Healthy wetlands are vital not only to the plants and animals that call them home but also to human populations. Running parallel to the Kootenay River, these wetlands act as storage tanks when water levels are high, providing flood control for the nearby city of Creston. Wetlands also purify and feed groundwater sources. The conservation effort involved in protecting this wildlife management area is no small feat. Active wetland management, continuous research and hard work keep these wetlands healthy.

Glacier National Park

Rugged mountains surrounded by cedar rainforest demonstrate the important role glaciers play in shaping landscapes

What Makes This Hot Spot Hot?

- Views of glacial recession shaping the landscape are available on many of the park's scenic hikes.
- Rogers Pass, where the Canadian Pacific Railway found its way through the towering Selkirk Mountains, is a National Historic Site.
- The park encompasses part of the oldest inland old-growth cedar rainforest in the world.

Address: 9520 Trans-Canada Hwy (Hwy 1), Rogers Pass, BC
Tel.: (250) 837-7500
Website: www.pc.gc.ca/en/pn-np/bc/glacier

GPS Coordinates
Latitude: 51.30403
Longitude: –117.52388

Open year-round, though trails may be inaccessible for hiking during the winter

🚶 🔭 🏊 ⛺

♿ (Check ahead)

↗ **Fireweed is a nitrogen-fixing plant often found in recently disturbed areas, making soil habitable for new plant life.**

This park holds a special place in Canadian history as British Columbia's first national park. Rogers Pass runs through the centre of Glacier National Park. A natural low point between the highest peaks of the Columbia mountain range, it was the last puzzle piece in the Canadian Pacific Railway. The Abandoned Rails Trail features artifacts and interpretive historical signs from the site's earliest days. The Rogers Pass Discovery Centre is a valuable stop for information about the park's ecosystems and history, including the important role the park played in mountaineering.

Glacier National Park shares the world's oldest inland old-growth cedar rainforest with Mount Revelstoke National Park. The Hemlock Grove Boardwalk makes for a lovely stroll through this unique environment, with massive hemlock and cedar trees towering over the path.

A more difficult hike, the Great Glacier Trail is a must-do for the avid hiker. People often speak of ancient glacial events creating the land we see today. This 6.5-kilometre round trip allows visitors to see the erosion process in action. Although the Great Glacier is no longer visible from the trail, its impact does not go unseen. In fact, as the glacier recedes it continues to shape the landscape.

Fireweed is a common and beautiful sight at higher elevations, particularly in areas just beginning to support plant life. The plant has beautiful pink flowers and is responsible for fixing nitrogen in the soil,

encouraging further plant growth. Western anemone is another magical sight in the alpine areas. It blooms as a small white flower in the spring, but by mid-summer it looks like a hairy puffball towering over other alpine flowers, such as the spotted saxifrage and bright monkeyflower.

At lower elevations, near the beginning of the trail, lush forests thrive on glacial runoff. As the trail gains elevation and nears the glacier, the landscape changes dramatically — a forest replete with rich vegetation becomes a rocky valley with talus slopes and patches of new vegetation. As of 2017 this glacier has receded over a kilometre since the late 1800s. More alpine and glacier viewing opportunities require trekking farther into the backcountry on trails, such as the steep but worthwhile Hermit Trail.

↑ It is easy to see the recent effects of glaciers in this rugged and mountainous landscape.

◂ Cinnamon black bears are sometimes seen roaming the wilderness.

Goat Range Provincial Park

Special grizzly bears saunter alongside clear alpine streams in this rugged wilderness

What Makes This Hot Spot Hot?

- The rare white-hued grizzly bear lives in this protected area, alongside mountain goats and other delightful forms of wildlife.
- The giant Gerrard trout spawns exclusively in this park, which makes this an important area for its survival.
- The park's rugged scree slopes and alpine meadows make it appealing to the backcountry naturalist.

Address: Accessible via forestry roads from Hwy 6 or Hwy 31, north of Kaslo, BC
Tel.: N/A
Website: www.env.gov. bc.ca/bcparks/explore/ parkpgs/goat_range

GPS Coordinates
Latitude: 50.23666
Longitude: −117.24643

Open year-round

As its name indicates, this park is a protective habitat for mountain goats, but it also holds many other gems. The rare white-hued grizzly bear can be found here and is recognizable by its blond coat, if a hiker is lucky enough to spot one from a distance. Woodland caribou, elk and small mammals, such as fishers, also wander this wild space. One may even hear the hoot of a short-eared owl in the winter and spring.

Below the surface of the Lardeau River is a highly important species for this area: the Gerrard rainbow trout. Goat Range Provincial Park contains the only waterways in which this trout spawns. It is an interesting species of fish because the males are particularly aggressive during spawning, meaning only the stronger and larger trout breed. As a result, the Gerrard trout has evolved to be very large. On average a spawning fish will be around 80 centimetres long.

From low to high elevations, old-growth stands of trees turn into alpine meadows with clear streams and scree slopes — all in one hike. The park is rugged and remote, greatly contributing to its beauty as a natural space. Within the park and immediate area are some amazing hikes. Hikers should be experienced, prepared and bear aware in this area. The only truly maintained hike within the park is the Wilson Falls Loop on the southern side. It is accessible by East Wilson Creek Forestry Service Road off of Highway 6 and leads to a spectacular waterfall through large cedar trees up to 1.5 metres in diameter. From the same road, the Alps Alturas Trail is a beautiful hike into exemplary alpine environs that feature scree slopes, white heather and alpine lakes. There are a number of other hikes in and around the park, including the spectacular Meadow Mountain. All the trails afford sensational wilderness-viewing opportunities.

→ **The Alps Alturas Trail is a wonderful way to experience the alpine.**

Halfway Hot Springs

A well-maintained campground with a natural hot spring that is close to recreational opportunities

What Makes This Hot Spot Hot?

- This spot boasts a true, natural hot spring experience in an area where you can find many developed hot springs.
- Many nearby hikes and birding opportunities make this campground a good home base after a day of adventures.
- A winter snowshoe followed by a dip in the hot pools is an experience not easily forgotten.

Address: The turnoff from Hwy 23 is 26 km north of Nakusp, BC. See the website below for specific details.
Tel.: N/A
Website: www.sitesandtrailsbc.ca/search/search-result.aspx?site=REC2279&type=Site

GPS Coordinates
Latitude: 50.50358
Longitude: −117.78373

Open year-round

A must-do on a tour of British Columbia hot springs, the Halfway Hot Springs are almost exactly halfway between Revelstoke and Nakusp. Surrounded by the beautiful trees and moss-covered roots of a riverside forest, this site is a perfect place for a relaxing camping trip. As the springs have become more popular, what used to be a rugged and difficult hike has become easier thanks to Recreation Sites and Trails BC. The hot springs are now a relatively established camping site with well-maintained trails and stairs. However, despite the site being well maintained, the road to the springs is still bumpy so a four-wheel drive vehicle is highly recommended.

For winter hot spring enthusiasts, snowshoeing is still necessary to reach the pools, but the winter trek there is well worth the effort as these geothermal springs are quite hot all year. Depending on the season hot spring users can adjust the temperature of the springs by tweaking how much hot spring water and cold water from the

Halfway River flow into the rocky pools. For instance, you may choose to add more hot water from a hose connected to the springs or more cold river water from another hose. When you are not relaxing in the pools, check out the forest trails around the springs or soak in the natural beauty along the riverside.

The surrounding area has been referred to as the Valley of Hot Springs, and it does live up to its name. Although the Halfway Hot Springs are the only accessible undeveloped springs, there are two well-known commercial hot springs nearby: Halcyon and Nakusp. The waters of all the springs eventually drain into the Arrow Lakes. What was once two widened areas in the Columbia River has essentially become one large lake following the building of a dam. The lakes are surrounded by wetlands and marshes as well as beautiful mountains and forests. If you feel the need to move out of relaxation mode there are many fantastic recreational opportunities nearby in the form of hiking, paddling and bird and wildlife watching.

↑ The river drains into the Arrow Lakes.

↖ Rocky pools hold spring water that has been heated far underground.

Kootenay National Park

Check out the park's unique Paint Pots before taking off on a scenic hike into the forest

What Makes This Hot Spot Hot?

- Forest succession following a fire in 2003 offers visitors a different visual experience every year.
- The Paint Pots, pools of spring water in ochre beds, are a geological beauty and traditional part of many First Nations cultures.
- Abundant in birds, mountain goats and even grizzly bears, this park is an ever-changing wildlife haven.

Address: Banff-Windermere Hwy (Hwy 93), north of Invermere, BC
Tel.: (250) 347-9505
Website: www.pc.gc.ca/en/pn-np/bc/kootenay

GPS Coordinates
Latitude: 50.974685
Longitude: −115.947277

Open year-round

♿ (Check ahead)

Excellent for a wide variety of short excursions, Kootenay National Park has a lot to offer, with relatively easy access. From glaciers to meadows and mineral baths, this park is an adventure waiting for you. A section of the Burgess Shale, which is an important fossil bed and another nature hot spot, lies in this park. Other main attractions are the Paint Pots, cold mineral spring pools sitting in beds of ochre. The shape and colour of the pools make one want to dip a large paintbrush in them! The Niitsitapi, Ktunaxa and Stoney Nations all collected ochre from this area to create paint for various purposes.

The park experienced five lightning wildfires in 2003, and the short Fireweed Loops take hikers on interpretive walks through a burned area. Fireweed and other plants are moving in rapidly and restoring nutrients to the soil. Hiking along these trails is a fantastic opportunity to see a recently burned forest growing and changing. The northern hawk owl, for which burned areas create new habitat, is already nesting and living here. Other species that will enjoy the forest as succession continues are grizzly bears and moose. Grizzlies love huckleberries, which generally appear at their best 25 years after a fire.

For something completely different, Marble Canyon Trail leads hikers to a river that cuts through a steep limestone and dolomite gorge, with spectacular mountain views en route. Keep an eye out and you may be lucky enough to spot a bighorn sheep.

With over 200 kilometres of trail, some just off the road and others deep into the backcountry along glaciers and up mountains, this park has something for everybody. And all visitors can agree that an ideal day of fun exploring the park finishes with a soak in the warm waters of Radium Hot Springs.

↗ **Fireweed is a common feature of the alpine as well as one of the first plants to regrow in areas affected by forest fires.**

→ **The northern hawk owl enjoys the habitat created by the park's 2003 fire.**

→ **The Paint Pots sit in ochre beds.**

WHITESWAN LAKE PROVINCIAL PARK

Lussier Hot Springs

These hot springs offer chances to watch wildlife right from the rocky pools

What Makes This Hot Spot Hot?

- Mineral-rich heated water seeps out of the earth and flows between rocky pools into a frigid river.
- Belted kingfishers are one of many birds that call this forest home and may dart out of the trees as you soak in the serene wilderness.
- Wildlife watching opportunities abound, and camping is available on nearby lakes.

Address: Whiteswan Lake Provincial Park, 17 km east on Whiteswan Lake Forest Service Road off Hwy 95, East Kootenay, BC
Tel.: (250) 422-3003
Website: www.env.gov. bc.ca/bcparks/explore/parkpgs/whtswan

GPS Coordinates
Latitude: 50.13515
Longitude: −115.5768

Open year-round

Natural, undeveloped hot springs alongside a river make for a relaxing experience. The hot springs are situated in Whiteswan Lake Provincial Park, where there is no shortage of wildlife. A quick hike off of the forestry service road leads to a little paradise. The benefits of these serene springs have been known to the Ktunaxa Nation for at least 5,000 years. They used the surrounding area as a seasonal hunting ground. When trappers, prospectors and guides arrived they began soaking in the waters after long days of hard work. The water can be as hot as 43 degrees Celsius, but cools as it flows between pools. And if you do overheat there is a frigid river right next to the springs that will cool you down.

Dense forest surrounds the river and protects moose, mountain goats and bears, both black and grizzly varieties. Keep an eye out for the belted kingfisher, one of a few bird species in which the females are more colourful

than the males, as well as other birds around the river or in the nearby lakes and forests. As you relax, look up and you may just spot a bald eagle soaring overhead.

A hot spring enthusiast with a sharp nose may notice a slight egg odour. As the water flows and is heated underground it becomes rich in minerals, such as sulphur. The smell is not the sulphur itself, but a gas produced by sulphur-eating bacteria deep underground. The water is harmless to bathe in so go ahead and relax in the serene pools while soaking in the surrounding wilderness. In the winter, enclosed by snow-covered trees that muffle the sounds of the forest, the steaming baths provide a completely different experience.

Basic toilets and changing rooms are available at the parking area. Just past the springs, Alces Lake offers camping facilities, and both Alces and Whiteswan lakes provide canoeing, swimming and more wildlife watching opportunities.

↑ The Lussier River, as seen from the hot springs.

↖ The female belted kingfisher is a rarity among birds as she is more colourful than her male counterpart.

Mount Revelstoke National Park

Alpine flowers bloom in open meadows that showcase the serenity of mountain life

What Makes This Hot Spot Hot?

- Visitors can travel from the farthest inland cedar rainforest in the world to a mountain summit within an hour.
- The alpine tundra, a high-altitude, treeless environment, supports a wide variety of wildflowers in the late summer.
- Birders have an opportunity to see three true alpine birds: the golden eagle, rosy finch and American pipit.

Address: Revelstoke, BC
Tel.: (250) 837-7500
Website: www.pc.gc.ca/en/pn-np/bc/revelstoke

GPS Coordinates
Latitude: 51.06815
Longitude: −117.97119

Open year-round with some road restrictions

↑ **A pika feeds on the alpine vegetation.**

↖ **Delicate pink monkeyflower flourishes in the alpine tundra.**

Move from the farthest inland cedar rainforest in the world to alpine tundra in a short, scenic drive to the Meadows in the Sky Parkway. Breathtaking viewpoints and short interpretive walks along the way make the drive alone worth the trip. Once at the parking lot you will notice a stunning display of alpine wildflowers. With the height of the bloom taking place in early August, look for the delicate white mountain-heather — with its small, white bell-shaped flowers — amid red paintbrush, pink monkeyflower, mountain arnica and spotted saxifrage, which is characterized by small yellow, orange and pink dots arranged on white petals.

Take a short stroll on a hemlock-shaded loop trail leading to Balsam Lake, or enjoy the informative First Footsteps Trail, which loops through hemlock groves and subalpine meadows with unforgettable views of the surrounding Monashee and Selkirk mountains. The trail features sculptures, artwork and interpretive signs

from the Secwepemc and Okanagan First Nations.

To experience true alpine tundra, a short uphill hike on the Upper Summit Trail will take you to the top of Mount Revelstoke. The golden eagle, rosy finch and American pipit are three true alpine birds found in this park, making this trek potentially very rewarding.

Hikes to Eva and Jade lakes can be done as long days — 6- and 13-kilometre round trips, respectively — or overnight camping trips. These less-travelled trails meander through hemlock forests, meadows blanketed in alpine flowers and scree fields. Watch for the pika, a small mammal inhabiting the rocky slopes of the alpine. A cousin of the rabbit with small, round ears,

the pika is very sensitive to climate change. As temperatures increase they flee to higher altitudes. Stay on the trail and respect the park's rules so as to preserve the food sources and remaining habitat of this high-altitude critter.

⬆ **Wildflowers bloom in abundance in tranquil meadows.**

◤ **Jade Lake is a popular campsite for backcountry campers.**

Premier Lake Provincial Park

A popular and easily accessed fishing hole in a gorgeous landscape

What Makes This Hot Spot Hot?

- A number of clear, emerald lakes are surrounded by trails and beautiful scenery.
- Well known for its fishing, this park has plenty of life in the water, including rainbow trout and western painted turtles.
- In the fall, larch trees turn yellow and shed their needles in green forests of Douglas-fir.

Address: Skookumchuck, BC
Tel.: (250) 422-3003
Website: www.env.gov.bc.ca/bcparks/explore/parkpgs/premier

GPS Coordinates
Latitude: 49.90983
Longitude: –115.64895

Open year-round

♿ (Check ahead)

Known for its fishing opportunities, Premier Lake Provincial Park is settled in the Rocky Mountains and named for the large body of water in its north end. First used as a fishing site by the Ktunaxa Nation, Premier Lake is still one of the most popular fishing lakes in the Kootenays. For those wanting to learn more about the fish in the lake, there is a fish ladder with interpretive signs about the life cycles of the resident rainbow trout close to the southern end of the lake.

The park has four other lakes close by, meaning there is no lack of places to explore. Douglas-fir and western larch trees line the banks of the park's emerald-coloured lakes. In the fall the needles of the larch turn yellow, a stunning contrast to the water and surrounding forests. We tend to associate falling leaves with deciduous trees, and although larch trees have needles they are in fact deciduous and drop their yellowing needles in time for the winter.

The Premier Lake Trail is a must-do loop that guides visitors through meadows and forests and connects Premier Lake to three other lakes. At Turtle Lake the western painted turtle is often seen sunning itself on logs just out of the water. If you visit in the late spring watch your step, as the female turtles journey out of the water to find a nice spot to lay their eggs. Some of these turtles have been known to go over 100 metres away from water to lay their eggs! In the winter the turtles burrow into the soft sediment on the lake bottom and hibernate until warmer weather. The trail continues through more beautiful landscapes with stops at Yankee and Canuck lakes. A separate trail leads visitors to Quartz Lake, a favourite local swimming spot. Always watch for birds and other wildlife on your hike. The nearby Premier Ridge is an important space for wintering herds of elk, deer and bighorn sheep.

→ **The waters of Premier Lake Provincial Park are surrounded by a breathtaking mountainscape.**

← **Western painted turtles sunbathe on logs around Turtle Lake.**

Top of the World Provincial Park

The lakes and meadows of this alpine plateau are sights you do not want to miss

What Makes This Hot Spot Hot?

- An easy hike in affords days of exploration through meadows, forests and true alpine landscapes.
- The spectacular base camp at Fish Lake hosts many birds, including osprey, which occasionally swoop from the trees to catch trout from the lake.
- Alpine flowers blanket fields in shades of purple, red and yellow.

Address: To access the trailhead turn east 4.5 km south of Canal Flats and follow about 50 km of forest service roads.
Tel.: (250) 489-8540
Website: www.env.gov.bc.ca/bcparks/explore/parkpgs/top_world

GPS Coordinates
Latitude: 49.88528
Longitude: −115.46989

Open year-round

The trails in Top of the World Provincial Park are fairly flat and easy for legs both short and long, making a trip to this alpine area a remote but family-friendly outdoor expedition. Fish Lake is the main access point and hub of activity for most visitors. Spectacular hike-in campsites and a shared backcountry cabin are a great home base from which to explore the landscapes surrounding the lake. With forests, meadows and mountain peaks close by one could stay at this campsite and hike for days! The trails surrounding Fish Lake are all relatively flat but still give guests a sense of being in an alpine environment.

Fish Lake supports a large bird population. Pine grosbeaks and boreal chickadees sing in the forest, while the distinct call of the common

loon echoes over the lake. When trout are spawning in the lake a bald eagle or osprey may swoop down from the trees to grab a meal just beneath the water's surface. As you venture away from the lake, alpine wildflowers bloom in meadows. Mule deer are common sights in the alpine meadows, where flowers, such as the red paintbrush and broadleaf arnica, paint the grassy fields red and yellow. Since the majority of the park is at a high elevation the trees are typical of alpine and sub-alpine environments. As the elevation increases, the trees gradually disappear, leaving hikers with panoramic views of the surrounding mountains.

While hiking in or out of the park, take a detour and look for Crazy Creek and Crazy River, places where flowing water abruptly appears out of the rocks. Water has dissolved the limestone bedrock and created underground channels through which the creek and river flow before they suddenly appear. Another geological feature of importance in this park is chert, which the Ktunaxa Nation used to make tools and weapons. Chert is a tough sedimentary rock, which forms sharp edges when chipped. Chert from this plateau was highly valued and traded extensively.

↑ A serene, lake-side morning in Top of the World Provincial Park.

← An osprey catches a trout just beneath the water's surface.

Valhalla Provincial Park

Hikers must prepare to feel an overwhelming sense of awe at the outstanding scenery

What Makes This Hot Spot Hot?

- It takes multiple visits to explore this varied park, from its alpine peaks to its lakeside forests.
- High in the alpine environs, mountain goats munch on grass in open fields near rocky slopes, while in the lower-elevation forests, grouse flutter between large trees.
- Pictographs from the Sinixt Nation alongside beautiful lakeshore campsites make canoeing an excellent way to explore the waters.

Address: The park is accessible by a number of trailheads and forest service roads as well as by boat from Slocan, Silverton and New Denver, BC
Tel.: N/A
Website: www.env.gov.bc.ca/bcparks/explore/parkpgs/valhalla

GPS Coordinates
Latitude: 49.8787
Longitude: −117.57156

Open year-round

The Valhalla Range of the Selkirk Mountains is nestled between the Arrow and Slocan lakes and protects an impressive array of wildlife and habitats. The elevation range enclosed in this protected area means wildlife can move through an entire watershed, from the slightest trickle of snow melting on a mountain to a rushing river or waterfall entering a lake.

The breathtaking scenery of the park is what draws many backcountry campers, hikers and canoeists. Spotting mountain goats as they make their way down steep rocky slopes on a misty morning is truly a magical sight. The park's landscape is characterized by jagged rocky spires, calm alpine lakes surrounded by serene meadows and dense forests of many tree species, including western redcedar and hemlock. Huckleberries grow close to the moss-covered forest floor at lower elevations. Higher up, blackberries, heather and grasses dominate the landscape

between forested areas.

Each environment provides a niche for different wildlife. Grizzly and black bears, lynx, bobcats, otters and a wide variety of other mammals inhabit various regions of the park. For birders, golden eagles and white-tailed ptarmigans frequent the alpine areas, while grouse, songbirds and waterfowl are abundant throughout the park.

The Gwillim Lakes area is a recommended destination for backcountry hikers and campers. At the end of a beautiful trail through amazing alpine forests and along lakes, the Gwillim Lakes themselves are absolutely stunning.

The park is well known by hikers and mountain bikers, but canoeing along the lakeshore of Slocan Lake is another pleasant way to experience the park. There are even marine campsites along the shoreline for those looking to do overnight kayak or canoe trips. Look for pictographs from the Sinixt First Nation as you paddle the shoreline.

↑ **The Gwillim Lakes area is a gorgeous destination with a scenic trail.**

↖ **Lucky visitors may spot a lynx from the trails.**

Index

Photo Credits